PLANNING FOR PEOPLE

Shopping Centres

A Developer's Guide to Planning and Design

by R I Northen FRICS

M Haskoll FRIBA ARIAS FFB

CENTRE FOR ADVANCED LAND USE STUDIES
COLLEGE OF ESTATE MANAGEMENT

PLANNING FOR PEOPLE

General Editors

Ian Northen FRICS (Director of Capital & Counties Property Company Limited)

John Leonard BSc ARICS (Director of CALUS)

Published March 1977
ISBN 090213233 4

Printed at the College of Estate Management
Whiteknights Reading RG6 2AW

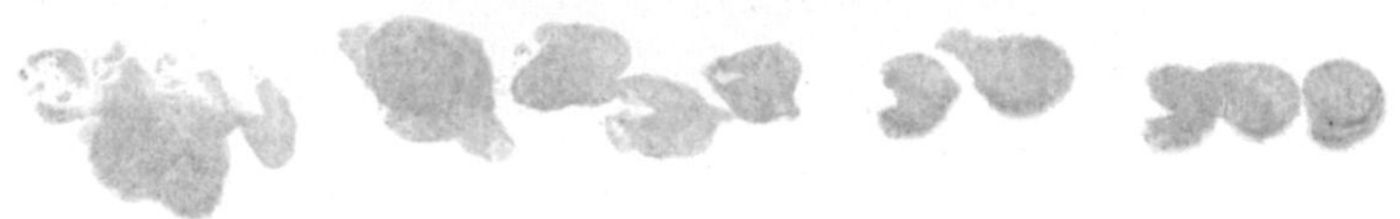

LIVERPOOL POLYTECHNIC LIBRARY
3 1111 00405 6840
WITHDRAWN

Foreword

By Mr R G A Lofthouse FRICS
Chairman of the Board of the College of Estate Management

One of the most marked features of the urban scene in the last two decades has been the emergence of new style shopping facilities in the form of pedestrianised streets, renovated arcades, in-town shopping centres, and out-of-town facilities such as hypermarkets. Representing as they do such an important element of the planning and development scene, it was natural that CALUS should build up a special interest in them, studying their form and impact from a variety of viewpoints, such as development and agency, subsequently progressing to research into more detailed aspects such as tenant mix and the requirements of those who have to occupy retail premises. With this steadily increasing involvement it was therefore understandable that when the opportunity arose for CALUS to be associated with this book on the subject of the management of shopping centres, the Board of the College should respond readily and warmly to the idea.

Mr Northen and Mr Haskoll have a very real practical experience of developing new shopping centres and it gives me considerable pleasure to introduce this book, in which the benefits of their experience are made so freely available to others.

R. G. A. Lofthouse

ACKNOWLEDGEMENTS

Acknowledgements

The authors and publishers also wish to acknowledge the co-operation and encouragement they have received from Capital and Counties Property Company Ltd, which has kindly made available its records, staff and experience in the preparation of this publication.

The authors appreciate the many helpful and constructive comments they have had from those who have kindly read through the early drafts of this publication. In particular, they wish to acknowledge the assistance and co-operation they have received from the staff of the Centre for Advanced Land Use Studies, including the untiring help, enthusiasm and advice which has been gratefully received from Patricia Davison.

The authors have made many references to shopping centres in various countries, and they wish to acknowledge the use of plans, photographs and other information which they have obtained from the following shopping centres.

Centre	Owner/Developer	Architect
Belle Epine Paris	SECAR	Cabinet Colloc et Philippe/Lathrop Douglas
Brent Cross London	Hammerson Property & Investment Trust Ltd	B E T Partnership
Carrefour Laval Montreal	The Fairview Corporation	
Coventry	The City of Coventry	The City Architect
Creteil France	SEMAEC	M Dufav
Eastgate Mall Hamilton	Cadillac Development Corporation	
Eastridge Regional Shopping Centre San José, California	HART Properties	Avner Naggar A/AArch
Eglington Square Toronto	Monarch Investments Ltd	J E Hoare Jnr
Eldon Square Newcastle upon Tyne	Capital & Counties Property Co Ltd, in association with the City of Newcastle upon Tyne	Chapman Taylor Partners
Esplanade Oxnard, California	John S Griffith & Co	Burke Kober Nicolais & Archuleta
Exton Square Pennsylvania	Exton Square Inc c/o the Rouse Co	Katzman Associates Inc
Four Seasons Mall Greensboro	Imperial Corporation	Valand Benzing & Associates
Franklin Park Shopping Centre Toledo, Ohio	J C Penney Co Inc	Charles L Barber & Associates

Centre	Owner/Developer	Architect
Galeries d'Anjou Montreal	Lakeshore Shopping Plaza Ltd	Bregman & Hamann
Ghirardelli Square Shopping Centre San Francisco	Lurline R Roth & William M Roth	Wurster Bernardi & Evans
Grigny 2 Paris	Société des Centres Commercieux	Cabinet Balick
Harlow New Town	Harlow Development Corp	Harlow Development Corp
Midtown Plaza Rochester, NY	B Foreman Co & McCurdy Co Inc	Victor Gruen
Old Orchard Chicago	Urban Investment & Development Co	Loebl, Schloiswann, Bennet & Dart
Parly 2 Paris	Société des Centres Commercieux	Lathrop Douglas
Place Bonaventure Montreal	Concordia Estates Ltd	R R Nicolet & Associates
Place Ville Marie Montreal	Trijec Equities Ltd	I M Pei & Associates
Pointe Claire Montreal	Lakeshore Shopping Plaza Ltd	Bregman & Hamann
Pyrford (neighbourhood shopping centre) Surrey		
Roosevelt Field Shopping Centre New York	Roosevelt Nassau Operating Corporation	I M Pei & Associates
Rosny 2 Paris	Société des Centres Commercieux	CNI International
Scarborough Town Centre Toronto	Trijec Equities Ltd	Greenspoon, Freelander, Plachta & Kryton
Sherway Gardens Toronto	Sherway Centre Ltd	Murray & Fleiss/Cranfield Stephens & Associates
Square One Montreal	The Fairview Corporation	
Velizy 2 Paris	Société des Centres Commercieux	Cabinet Petar Copeland
Victoria Centre Nottingham	Capital & Counties Property Co Ltd	Arthur Swift & Partners
Waltham Cross London	Electricity Supply Nominees Ltd	Richard Shepherd Robson & Partners
Woodfield Mall Chicago	The Taubman Co Inc/ Sears Roebuck	Jickling & Lyman
Yorkdale Toronto	Trijec Equities Ltd	Trijec/John Graham Consultants

Contents

1 Preface

This may seem a strange time to consider the planning and design of shopping centres when so few are likely to be started in the immediate future. Nevertheless, new centres and refurbishment schemes will be undertaken again sooner or later. A lull in development activities may in fact be a convenient time to review what we have learned in the past decade so that new schemes, when they come, may have the benefit of past experience. With the Community Land Act 1975 now in operation and a new attitude to development beginning to appear, the present may be a particularly opportune time to attempt to record the planning principles, design techniques and development procedures which the authors believe are now firmly established in practice, although not generally set down in text-books.

DEFINITIONS

Many terms relating to shopping centres are in day-to-day use. While their meanings are generally understood, there is no standard book of reference providing detailed definitions of them, and the following glossary explains how some of these terms are used in this book. (In preparing this list we have referred to recently published articles and reports, including those shown below.[1])

Convenience goods

These goods are purchased regularly, and therefore convenience of location, selection and buying are of importance to the shopper. In addition to food, these regular purchases include newspapers, cleaning and toiletry materials, tobacco, liquor, inexpensive clothing, hardware and electrical supplies.

Convenience shops include corner shops, supermarkets, superstores, and hypermarkets. The sales of the larger convenience shops are not confined to convenience goods but may well include a limited range of comparison goods.

Comparison goods (also known as **durable goods**)

Comparison goods are long term purchases made at irregular intervals, when suitability, quality, price and style are important factors in selection. Such goods are stocked in a wide range of sizes, colours, styles and qualities. They include clothing, footwear, fashion, jewellery, fabrics, furniture, garden equipment and the more expensive household equipment such as washing machines, refrigerators, freezers and vacuum cleaners. Comparison shopping is normally located in town and city centres where department and variety stores can offer a wide selection of goods. Although many comparison goods are taken away by the shopper, the larger, heavier items will be delivered.

Shop units

A shop unit is a retail unit with a selling space of less than 400 square metres (m^2) – 4 000 square feet (ft^2). This includes the majority of units occupied by both local and multiple traders, even where they occupy a double or treble unit of normal depth of up to about 20 metres (60 ft). The definition also includes units occupying less than about 15 m^2 (250 ft^2); these are generally known as kiosks.

Stores

Units larger than 400 m^2 (4 000 ft^2) of selling area are best termed 'stores' and may be sub-divided into the following categories:

1 'Hypermarkets'	The *Architects' Journal* 5 May 1976
Interim Shopping Policy	John Collins, County Planner, Cheshire County Council
The Future Pattern of Shopping	Distributive Trades Economic Development Council (HMSO 1971)

1 **Department stores**
These are defined in the 1971 Census of Distribution as having 25 or more employees and selling a wide range of commodities, including clothing and household goods. A department store offering a large selection of goods usually requires a selling space of more than 10 000 m^2 (100 000 ft^2) and possibly as much as 20 000 m^2 (200 000 ft^2). Examples of department store operators are the John Lewis Partnership, Debenham's, House of Frazer and Fenwicks.

2 **Variety stores** (sometimes known as **bazaar stores**)
These usually have a selling area of between 1 000 m^2 (10 000 ft^2) and 8 000 m^2 (80 000 ft^2) and sell a wide range of goods displayed in racks or trays for self-selection. They do not usually provide a delivery service. Examples include Woolworth, Littlewoods, British Home Stores[1] and Marks & Spencer[1].

3 **General household stores**
These are often similar in size to variety stores but tend to cover household, gardening and stationery requisites. Typical examples are Boots, Timothy White, W H Smith and Habitat.

4 **Specialist stores**
These cover a very wide range of selling areas (from 500 to 5 000 m^2) and concentrate mainly on fashion goods. Examples are Miss Selfridge, Chelsea Girl, Burtons (Top Shop), Austin Reed, Mothercare and C & A.

Supermarkets

These are self-service food shops having a minimum selling area of 400 m^2 (4 000 ft^2). Anything smaller than 400 m^2 but larger than 200 m^2 is known as a **superette.** Most larger operators now regard 400 m^2 (4 000 ft^2) as the minimum size, and it is generally accepted that 2 000 m^2 (20 000 ft^2) is the maximum unless a wide range of non-food goods is to be sold.

Cash and carry and other retail warehouses

A wholesale warehouse is generally a building used for the storage of goods and bulk supply to retailers and merchants for the purposes of resale or manufacture.

A cash and carry warehouse is a building used both for storage and the sale of goods at a discount to both traders and members of the public.

There are other forms of retail warehouse which have a prime purpose of selling directly to the public, such as the catalogue or mail order warehouse.

Superstores

Shops or stores with a selling area greater than 2 500 m^2 (25 000 ft^2) are usually known as superstores. They normally operate on a single level in both peripheral and town centre locations with good car parking facilities. They offer a range of food products as well as a limited range of low priced non-food products. They are normally planned on a self-service basis with check-outs.

Maximum selling area for a superstore is usually 5 000 m^2 (50 000 ft^2). Examples of superstore operators are Asda, International, Fine Fare and Tesco.

Hypermarkets

Hypermarkets are always located away from town centres and occupy selling areas of more than 5 000 m^2 (50 000 ft^2). In addition to food they offer a wide choice of non-food goods. They are very dependent on the car shopper, and substantial open car parking facilities are essential — possibly as much as one car per 5 metres of selling space.

1 These could equally be described as specialist stores, as their main trade is fashion.

All planning applications for shops of more than 5 000 m^2 have to be referred to the Department of the Environment unless they are located in an established town or district centre. This effectively allows Government control over hypermarket locations.

The neighbourhood centre

This small centre is usually based on a supermarket and covers a wide range of convenience goods as well as some personal services such as laundry, dry cleaning and shoe repairs. 1

It normally has an area of about 5 000 m^2 (50 000 ft^2) and serves a population of 5 000 to 10 000 people. Its catchment area radius does not normally exceed five miles.

The district centre (or **community centre**)

The district centre is built around a small department store or a variety store as the principal tenant. 2
Its size range is usually from 10 000 m^2 (100 000 ft^2) to 30 000 m^2 (300 000 ft^2) and it services the needs of a catchment area of 10 000 to 150 000 people. In addition to convenience goods, it offers a range of comparison goods and personal services.

This type of centre is to be found as the main shopping centre for our small to medium-sized towns which cannot support a regional centre with department and variety stores.

The regional centre (town centre or down-town)

This is essentially a comparison trading centre (ie one visited on a monthly or occasional shopping trip 3
to buy goods such as fashion, shoes, furniture and electrical equipment, where price comparison is important), with a wide catchment area extending to a radius of 25 miles or more, depending on the standard of roads and public transport services. It is usually based on one or more department stores and offers a complete range of general merchandise, apparel, furniture and home furnishings.

Such a centre has a trading area of at least 30 000 m^2 (300 000 ft^2) and draws on a population of at least 150 000.

When considering a regional centre in relation to a central area, it is necessary to look at the overall retailing facilities to determine the general characteristics of the centre. Many small centres within the city may be really regarded simply as an addition to the overall shopping content. It is necessary to see whether there is a common pedestrian flow, for merely to build a new centre in the vicinity of an established area is not itself sufficient unless adequate provision of 'magnet' traders is made to generate a pedestrian flow into the new centre.

It must be recognised that many of the existing shopping centres within our larger towns and cities have the essential characteristics of a regional shopping centre and do in fact perform this function of providing the shopper with the choice of a very wide range of comparison goods. As they have developed gradually as a result of natural influences, the planning of such centres will vary tremendously.

The out-of-town or suburban centre

The out-of-town centre is now well established in North America, Australia and France. Brent Cross is 4
the first in the UK, but it is unlikely that it will be followed by others, at least for some years. Such centres depend upon land availability, a mobile and affluent population within a radius of say 25 miles, a good road system and the substantial financial resources to enable such a development to proceed. Regional suburban centres are normally anchored on at least two department stores as well as several variety and specialist stores. Although mainly comparison trading centres, they usually include a supermarket and some specialist food traders. There is a tendency for the food trading element to be located within one area of the centre or sometimes within a separate building adjacent to the car park.

Car parking facilities must be adequate, as these centres are almost completely dependent on the car shopper, unless public transport facilities are available. The American standard is 5:5 cars per 100 m^2 (1 000 ft^2) of gross leasable area.

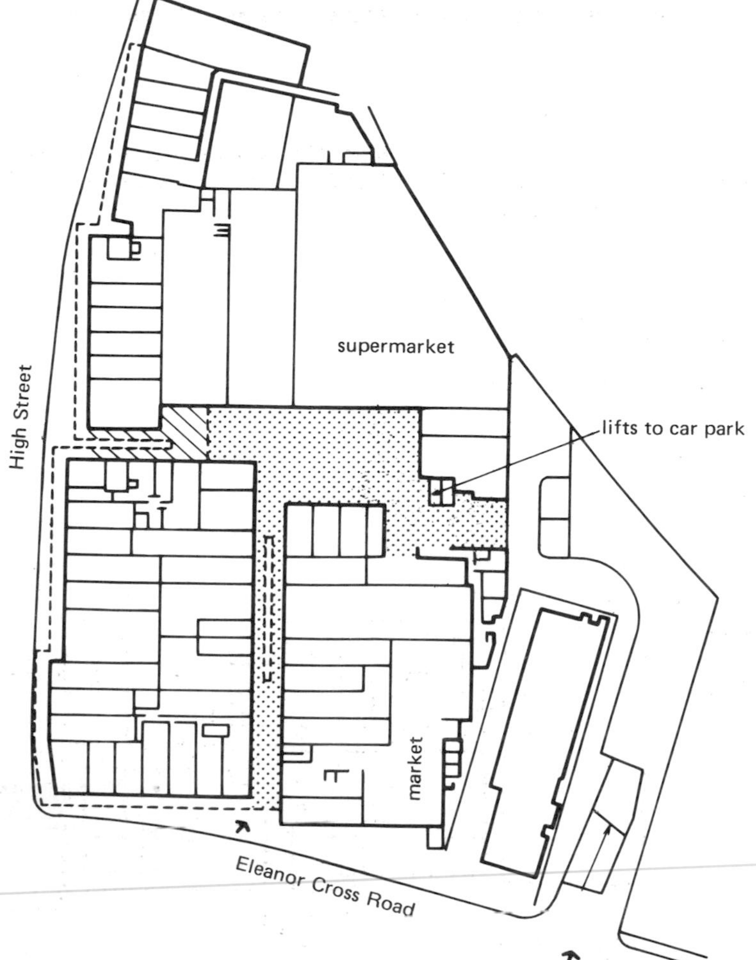

1 PYRFORD, SURREY
A neighbourhood shopping centre which is typical of many of the post-war period. They are usually based on a supermarket and sometimes include a variety store.

2 WALTHAM CROSS, HERTFORDSHIRE
A shopping centre based on a supermarket, which occupies the largest unit and therefore places the centre in the neighbourhood category. However, because of its close proximity to other shopping in adjacent streets, this development forms part of a district centre.

KEY TO PLANS THROUGHOUT

 *Pedestrian areas*

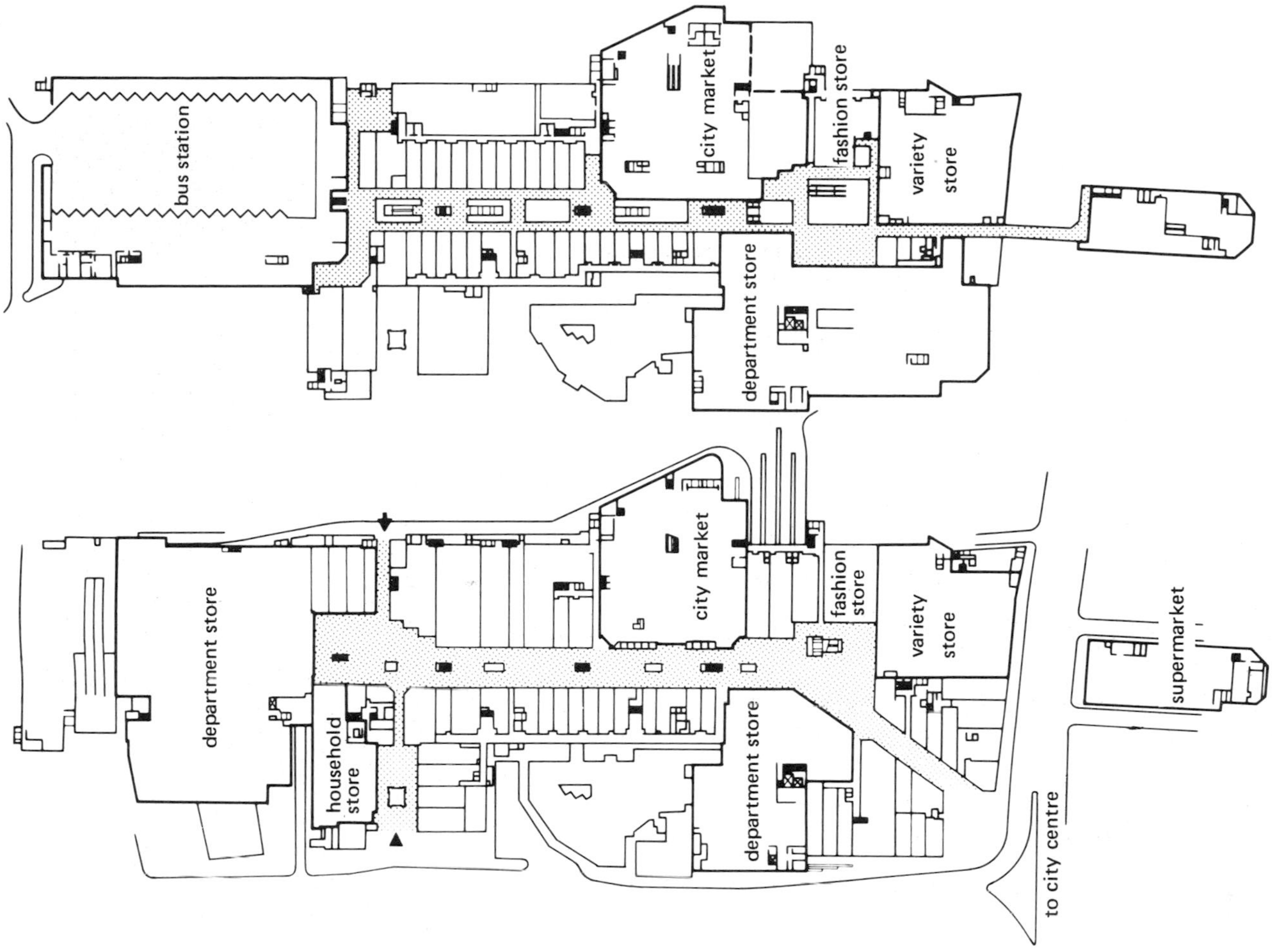

VICTORIA CENTRE, NOTTINGHAM 3

Possibly the first really successful covered two-level regional shopping centre in Britain. With its two department stores, its general household store, retail market, bus station and large underground car park, it has all the constituents of a regional centre, although in fact it developed periphery land and effectively extended the shopping centre of Nottingham.

BRENT CROSS, NORTH LONDON 4

The first British example of an out-of-town, car-orientated shopping centre. Note that it might be criticised for providing unnecessarily long frontages to the department and variety stores.

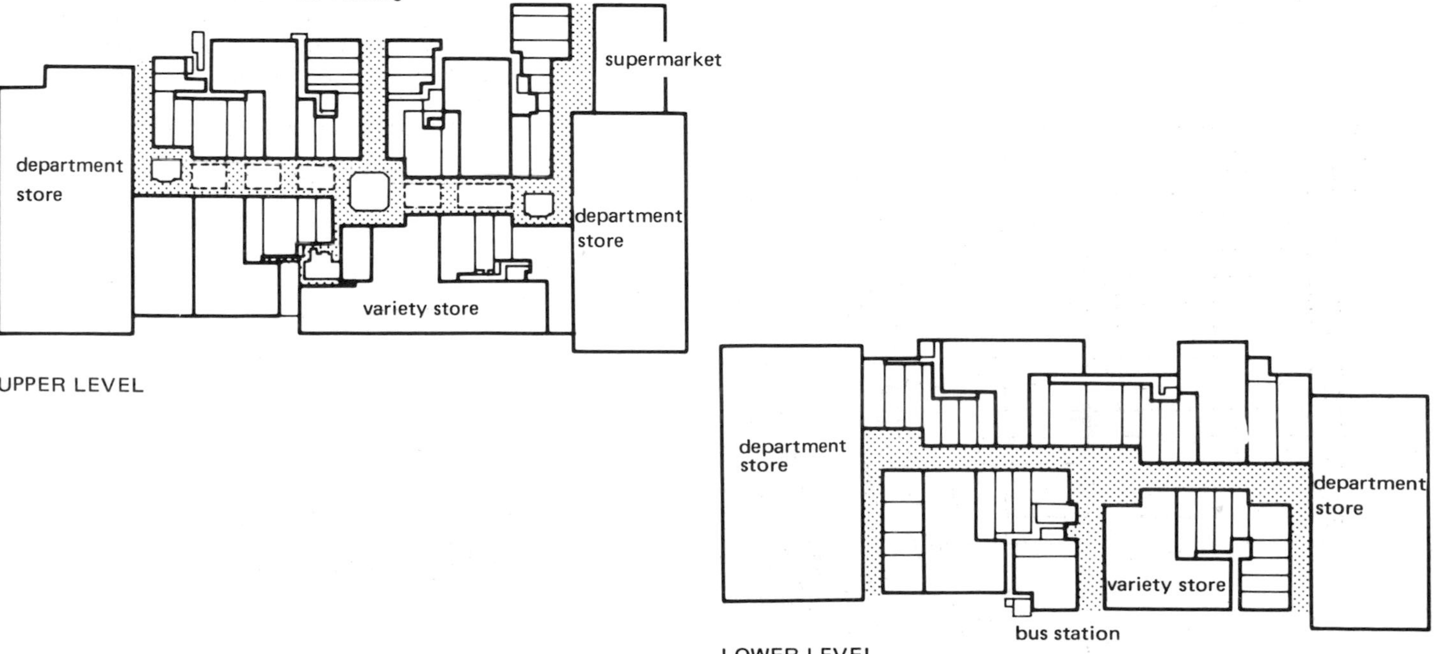

Service trades

A wide range of services is provided from retail units within shopping centres. They often require little frontage and sometimes occupy basement or non-selling floor space. Their location within a shopping centre requires very careful planning if their presence is not to be detrimental to pedestrian flow.

Typical examples are travel agents, building societies, banks, employment agencies, estate agencies, dry cleaners, betting offices and hairdressers.

Floor areas

For planning purposes, various definitions of floor area are used. The generally accepted interpretations are as follows:

1 **Selling floor area**
In relation to a shop or store, this is the total area of the space to which the public has access. It would include the sales area, entrance, vestibule and public toilets.

2 **Net sales area**
This is the selling area to which the public has access. Entrance, vestibules, public toilets, storage and staff areas are excluded. The term normally refers to the area used by retailers to calculate the sales density of their trading turnover.

3 **Gross retail area**
This is the total floor area measured up to the perimeter of the external walls. In relation to a shop unit, it would include storage, food preparation, selling floor area, staff accommodation and plant rooms. When related to the total shopping centre, the accommodation included within this description usually needs to be specified in detail to show whether malls, lift lobbies, bus stations, service roads, covered car parks, market halls and plant areas are included.

4 **Gross leasable area**
Within a shopping centre, this is the total floor area occupied by retailers. It thus excludes common areas such as malls, service roads, and car parks, but includes market halls. Where ancillary facilities are included in the centre such as flats, offices, bus stations, recreational centre, bingo halls and cinemas, it is preferable to specify these areas separately.

Shopping arcade

A covered narrow pedestrian way, with shops on either side, having sufficient width only for shoppers to pass, and without space for seating, planting and other furniture. Arcades often provide a convenient pedestrian link between busy thoroughfares. Traditionally, the shops fronting the arcade are the small specialist boutiques and kiosks, although more recent arcade developments have often been planned with standard shop units.

An arcade is normally 4.5 - 6 metres (15-20 ft) wide. Examples are Burlington Arcade, Piccadilly, London; and Place Ville Marie, Montreal.

Shopping mall

The use of the word 'mall' to describe a pedestrianised shopping street almost certainly originated in North America in an effort to convey a greater sense of space, quality and elegance than is normally associated with an arcade. Malls are usually covered and wide enough to provide a central area for planting, seating, fountains and other furniture. Although shops fronting an arcade are usually smaller than those in a shopping mall, the basic difference between a mall and an arcade lies not in the types of shops found in them but in the volume of space between the facing frontages.

A mall consists of some 3 - 3.5 metres (10-12 ft) of clear walking space in front of the shops on either side, and a central reservation of some 4 - 8 metres (13-26 ft). The total width of the mall therefore would be in the order of 10 - 15 metres (33-50 ft). Examples are the Victoria Centre, Nottingham; Yorkdale, Toronto; and Parly 2, Paris.

2 Introduction

'Shopping for pleasure'

In 1969 the joint authors of this publication collaborated in *Shopping for Pleasure* which was produced by Capital & Counties Property Company Limited. The continuing demand for this document has encouraged them to update and expand it into a form particularly helpful to local authorities, consultants and students who are interested in property development. The present book is intended, therefore, as the first of a series of guides on the subject of property development. The series will be an attempt to bring together the technical knowledge and the practical experience of the property developer, and will cover (among others) such matters as:

Real estate aspects of shopping centres
Partnerships with local authorities
Management of shopping centres
Project management of developments

In preparing these publications, a variety of specialists will contribute their development, local authority and professional consultancy experience.

It is hoped that this information, which has been largely accumulated in the painful school of practical experience, will at least help those about to embark on major development projects to avoid some of the pitfalls with which many developers have had to contend in the past.

Prospects for new shopping centres

It is unlikely that in the immediate future any developer or local authority will take on a new capital commitment for a shopping centre. Indeed, in some recent instances developers have been obliged to withdraw from central area redevelopment schemes such as those at Cardiff, Staines, Kidderminster, Middlesbrough and others, even at the expense of abandoning expenditure to date or, in the case of Cardiff, paying the city some £3m in compensation. Even where schemes are viable at present interest rates, the capital resources are unlikely to be available. Nevertheless, new developments will eventually start up again even if, in the short and medium term, the more ambitious enclosed shopping centres have to be abandoned in favour of more modest concepts. Careful planning and efficient development will be essential if capital resources are limited, and this book may make some contribution to achieve that end, for whatever the type of shopping centre, the basic problems, such as pedestrian flow and tenant mix, will always apply.

A further difficulty facing the large enclosed air-conditioned centre is the increasingly high cost of labour, fuel, cleaning, security, etc, which produce high service charges. Such centres must be able to attract sufficient shoppers to achieve the necessary additional turnover to compensate the trader. They must also be managed prudently and skilfully to ensure that tenants get good value for money. Nevertheless, the quality of the environment and the safety, convenience and comfort of these centres will certainly make them infinitely more attractive to most shoppers than the average high street — which may be noisy, untidy and dangerous. Quite often, the high street cannot find the space to accommodate the larger retailers. A typical indication of the growing popularity of the modern enclosed shopping centre may be taken from the car parking usage figures at the Victoria Centre, Nottingham, which are as follows:

1973	958 460 cars	(There has also been a significant
1974	1 088 437 "	increase in the average length of
1975	1 124 657 "	stay per car)

Successful centres which have been built in the relatively cheap building cost era prior to 1976 will enjoy a monopoly position for some years ahead. A national shortage of capital resources will provide an effective restraint on the creation of competing centres.

The role of property development companies

In the past, major development companies have provided the funds for development as well as the benefit of technical expertise and experience. Considerable uncertainty exists at present as to the extent to which local authorities will rely on property development companies to assist them under the Community Land Act. Development companies undoubtedly have a major contribution to make if they can be given the opportunity, although this could well centre on the provision of expertise rather than finance. Over the last decade at least, many developers have acquired considerable knowledge of the design and construction of most types of commercial development. Further, they have probably learned to minimise the risk element and to obtain reasonable control over building cost and contract time.

Perhaps an aspect of development that is often ignored or under-estimated is the problem of dealing with people. Controlling numerous consultants, contractors, retailers and shoppers requires diplomacy, patience, tact and great determination. Developers who have created major schemes and successfully managed extensive portfolios must have acquired most of these qualities if they have managed to maintain a satisfactory public image. Property development companies such as Ravenseft, Town & City, Hammersons and Capital & Counties have all undertaken developments amounting to many millions of pounds, and their experience is well known to many local authorities and consultants. Details of many such shopping schemes are shown in the CALUS publication *Rent Assessment and Tenant Mix in Planned Shopping Centres* (published in September 1975).

The role of local authorities

In the past, shopping centre development was invariably instigated and financed by property development companies. Increasingly, however, local authorities wished to have a greater involvement in the development than could be achieved by the exercise of their powers as planning authority. Moreover, as schemes became larger it became clear that only in exceptional cases was it possible for a private developer to acquire a multiplicity of site interests necessary for a comprehensive redevelopment.

Consequently, in the case of larger town centre schemes it has for some time usually been the local authority which have initiated the development. Now, and for the foreseeable future, it seems inevitable that new shopping centres can only be provided if the local authority wish this to happen and have the determination to see that it does.

Occasionally local authorities have undertaken their own schemes without the assistance of a property development company. Whilst some may have found this worth-while, others have subsequently had good reason to regret taking this course; but where local authorities do proceed independently of a property development company, then the references in this publication to the developer are just as relevant to the local authority which is acting in the role of a developer. For most local authorities, however, it is prudent to bring in a property development company, for the following reasons:

- i Few authorities have sufficient staff with the requisite technical qualifications and development experience
- ii The committee organisation of the local authority can be too inflexible for quick decision making
- iii Local government officers cannot usually advise their councils to take decisions involving an element of risk which is quite commonly accepted in a commercial undertaking.

Most property development companies with an established track record have paid quite dearly for their commercial development experience, and have moreover accumulated considerable knowledge in design trends, project management, tenant mix, leasing centre management etc. This in itself is, of course, no guarantee for success, as numerous schemes involving development companies have all too often turned out to be dismal failures. When this has happened it has frequently resulted from a failure either in the procedure for the selection of the developer or in the basis of his appointment.

The role of the local authority will depend on the size and character of the project as well as the capacity of the local authority to play an effective part in the development team. In many circumstances their officers will act as equal partners with the developer in the development team.

The basis for appointing a developer

There has often been too much readiness on the part of local authorities to accept the highest initial ground rent offered by a developer, and insufficient importance has been attached to the benefit of using a company of proven experience as a developer.

A building contractor is nowadays reluctant to quote a fixed price for a building, even where plans and bills of quantity are available and construction is imminent. Even assuming a return to the times when developers were competing with each other for local authority developments, it is therefore probably unrealistic to expect a developer to quote a minimum ground rent for a development which has not been planned in detail and which may not be constructed for several years hence, by which time interest rates, building costs and rental levels may have fluctuated quite dramatically.

Both the local authority and the developer must have reasonable flexibility to review the terms of the partnership if there is a significant change in conditions. The parties may find themselves working together as partners or as landlord and tenant for the next ninety-nine years, and it is important that mutual trust and understanding are quickly established if a fund of goodwill is to be maintained. As every developer knows, the most straightforward developments are fraught with hazards which will test the strongest of relationships and on occasions even precipitate the withdrawal of the developer during the planning stages.

It is beyond the scope of this book to look in depth at the form of the relationship between developer and local authority. For the immediate future it looks as if the local authority, which is contributing the land element of the scheme, will expect a minimum ground rent together with a share in the equity of the development after the developer has been allowed an agreed basic return on the cost of the development.

The scope of the developer's contribution

To some extent the scope of the developer's contribution will depend on his particular experience and expertise. On a large or complex scheme it is vital that the developer should be appointed early enough to be involved in the selection of the professional consultants and to participate in the design brief. Once the development team has been established it will usually be the developer's function to control and co-ordinate its activities. Whilst the architect has traditionally led the design team, it is for the developer to ensure that solutions are reached which satisfy the often conflicting demands of good architecture, local authority building and Fire Officer requirements, as well as the needs of shoppers and retailers and the necessity for commercial viability.

The structure of the development team

One of the problems in achieving a satisfactory conclusion to any town centre development is that it is so complex and the number of interested parties so great, that considerable skill and strength of purpose is necessary to keep a balance between desirabilities and practicabilities. Even a private developer who can, when necessary, immediately make his own decisions may expect to take as long as ten years from concept to opening; so any authority relying on a committee structure must recognise that it is almost certain to take considerably longer, and even then they may fail in the end either to get a centre at all or to get a really good one.

The development team must consist of a relatively small number with whom effective management should rest. They must of course be answerable, but the development responsibility should be theirs.

For the Eldon Square development undertaken by Capital & Counties Property Company in partnership with the City of Newcastle upon Tyne, it was found necessary to set up a series of joint committees, each dealing with one aspect of development progress. Final decisions, however, were taken by a small policy committee comprising the three Chief Officers, the developer and the architect.

It is undesirable that any one member of the development team should dominate. This particularly applies where the architect has very strong views on the design concept, which may not necessarily be appreciated by the developer, let alone the shopper, who will only use the centre if she finds it attractive and convenient. In this connection, the role of the local authority should not be under-estimated. Officers can be very sensitive to local tastes, habits and attitudes, and the architect, who may not be locally based, should ensure that every opportunity is given to the authority to make a positive contribution in design and planning matters.

The shopping centre as a community centre

It will be one of the prime objectives of the local authority, the funding institution and the developer to ensure that a shopping centre is a success. No doubt the criteria for measuring success will vary according to the objectives of the party concerned. The local authority will want to ensure that the scheme does not put an undue burden on the rates, and will almost certainly wish to secure other non-commercial benefits such as pedestrianisation, off-street servicing, public libraries, car parking, recreation centres and similar planning benefits. The pension fund will wish to ensure that payments to pensioners are not prejudiced. The developer will have to see a fair return on risk capital merely to stay in business.

In spite of these varying objectives, most participants in a successful development will agree that one of their greatest satisfactions and rewards is to see the centre being used and enjoyed by people of all types, classes and ages. The attractive and well designed centre — perhaps containing restaurants, pubs, recreational centres, discotheques and sometimes cinemas — is not merely somewhere to do the weekend shopping but also a place where friends can meet and the family can spend its leisure time, and therefore where adequate facilities should be provided.

Very often a trip to the shopping centre is a pleasurable day's outing for an old age pensioner, who can take a 'free' bus into the shopping centre and spend a pleasant few hours, possibly buying very little but nevertheless enjoying the movement of shoppers and contact with other people under conditions of comfort and safety. In the larger enclosed centres it is usual to mount regular exhibitions in the malls to provide added interest. In the very largest centres there may be fountains, water features, decorative and musical clocks and play features, all of which can help to create an exciting and attractive environment.

In an earlier age, before we had our modern systems of rapid transport and mass communications, the town centre was both a market place and a meeting place. The modern shopping centre once again provides the opportunity for our town centres to be much more than merely soulless shopping high streets. They can and very often do provide a living heart for the community.

This book is concerned with the technicalities of achieving a successful shopping centre, and it might be criticised for implying that people should be thought of in an inhuman way. Others may take the view that shopping centres are wasteful of resources in seeking to persuade shoppers to buy goods they really do not want. Such criticisms would be unenlightened, for what this book sets out to illustrate is how shopping can be made attractive to people. A successful shopping centre will be part of community life, shared equally by shopper and shopkeeper. It will provide a framework in which both 'capitalist' and 'socialist' ideals are catered for. Not only will the shopkeepers find an opportunity to trade well, but the shoppers will also find the right environment to make up their minds, so that they can buy what they want with care and in comfort.

It is a waste of human endeavour to produce something which is not successful, and it is believed that normal human beings take a pride in being part of something that is. It is within this framework that those things which help to make something better have been technically and, it is hoped, rationally described.

In conclusion, it must be stressed that the shopper is the final arbiter of the success of the centre. If developers and planners can achieve a strong pedestrian flow, it is an indication that they have succeeded in making the centre attractive, convenient and efficient for both shopper and retailer. Unless they can create optimum shopping conditions for the retailer, there is little likelihood that the resources will be available to provide the shopper with the quality of environment in which shopping can truly be a pleasure.

3 Past experience

The growth of shopping centres in post-war Britain

In the years between the two world wars there was a
steady growth in the influence and strength of high
streets, in small towns as well as in large. Growth was
generally haphazard and took a linear form, the 5
shopping streets often becoming very extended and
forming tenuous links between established shopping
areas. The fragmented nature of site ownership
effectively prevented large scale redevelopment.

In the immediate post-war era there arose two major opportunities for rethinking the approach to the planning of shopping facilities in town centres. One was in the rebuilding of bomb damaged town centres, and the other was in the creation of new towns. Unfortunately, the underlying principles of shopping centre planning were not sufficiently well understood at that time for new ideas to be fully exploited, although there is really nothing very new or sophisticated in the basic concepts, which are now rather better known. An important factor which our planners failed to recognise early enough was the impact of the motor car both on the shopping environment and on the behaviour of the shopper.

OXFORD STREET, LONDON **5**
In spite of its inconvenience, due to lack of pedestrianisation and parking facilities, this is still one of the most popular shopping streets in the world, because it contains the 'magnet' stores and shops.

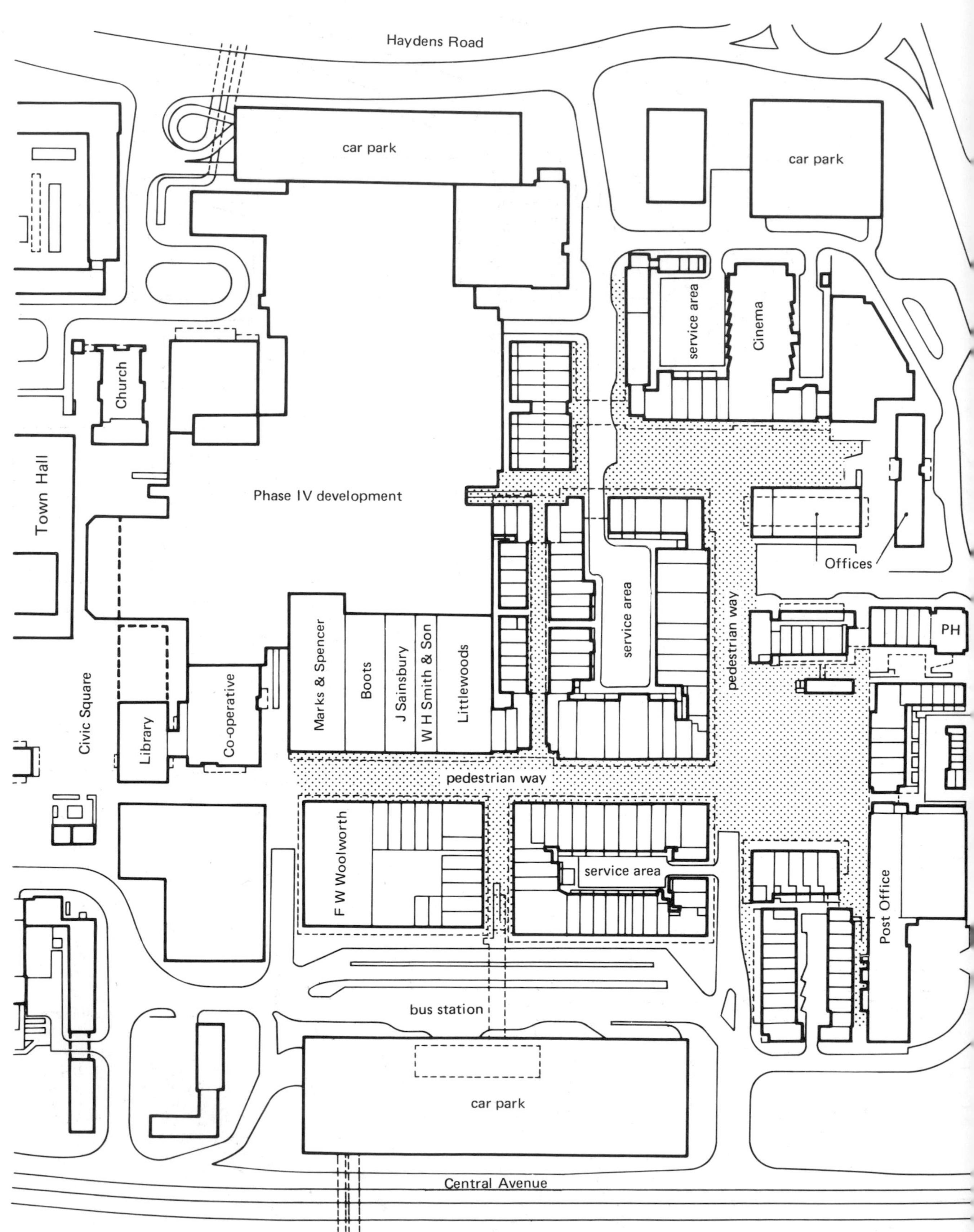

6 HARLOW, ESSEX
An example of a post-war new town shopping centre. They were uncovered and normally pedestrianised. Harlow was better than most, but there were none of the subtleties of pedestrian flow and siting of 'magnet' stores.

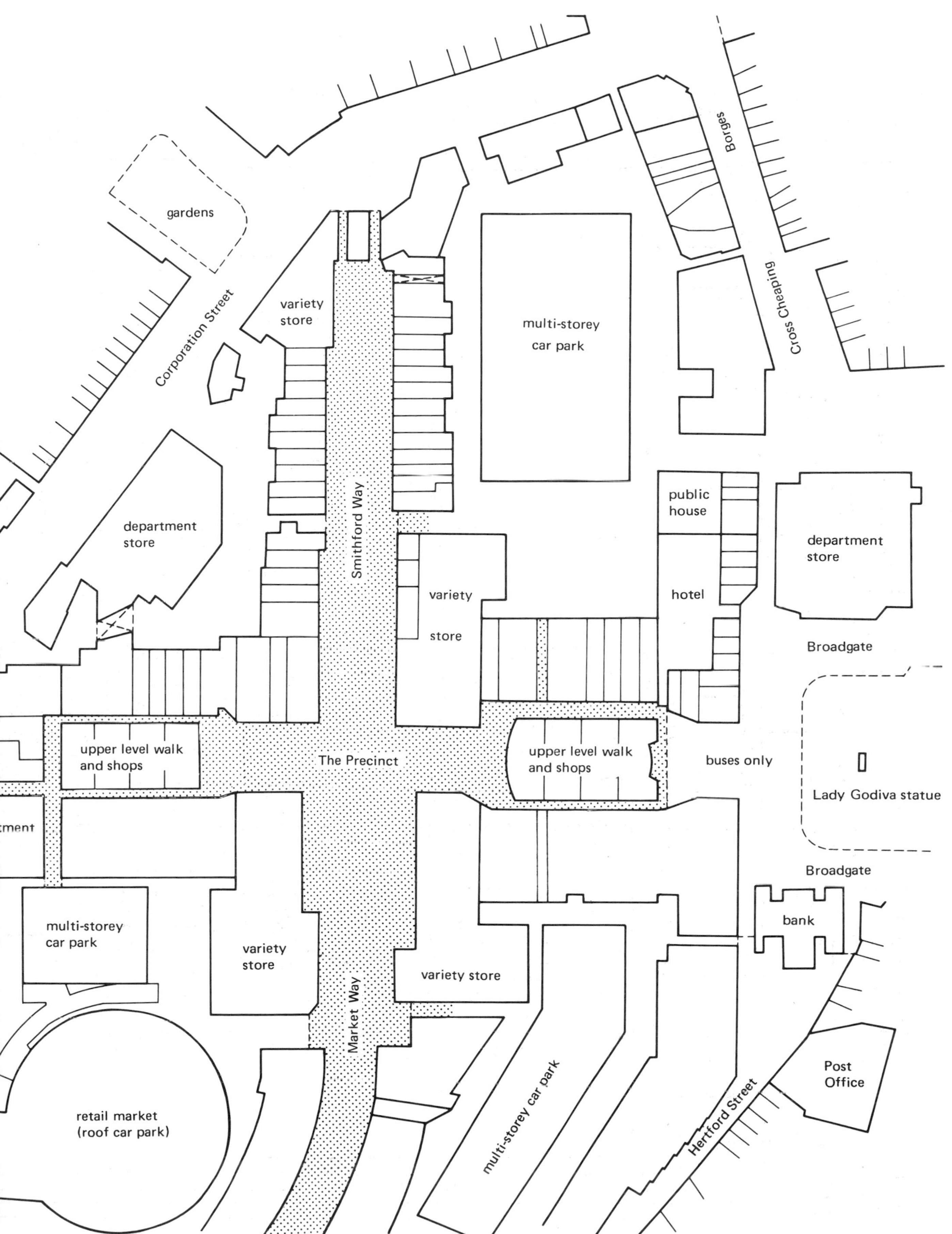

COVENTRY **7**

An early pedestrianised shopping centre, built as part of the post-war rebuilding of the bomb-damaged city.

Such retail developments as took place in the fifties and early sixties in cities such as Plymouth, Bristol, Swansea, Exeter and Southampton, as well as in the
6 earlier new towns like Crawley, Harlow and Hemel Hempstead, were modelled very much on pre-war concepts.

7 The city of Coventry provided one of the first attempts to plan a completely new form of shopping centre. It could hardly fail, as it had little effective competition. Nevertheless, few today would regard it as an effective solution in terms either of comfort, cleanliness and convenience for the shopper or of trading efficiency for the retailer. The problems of pedestrian flow and multi-level shopping were barely appreciated.

In the later sixties was built the first of the fully enclosed shopping centres, which introduced a new concept of shopping safety, comfort and convenience. Not unnaturally, however, some of the earlier attempts to design fully integrated shopping centres were mediocre and a few quite disastrous, both for the developer and for the community they served.

Although it must be conceded that the Americans, and latterly the French, have demonstrated more sophistication and more experience in this field, the special situation in the UK ensures nevertheless that only the very worst of our new centres will not succeed commercially, for our planning and transport system insulates new centres from competition with other centres. Most American housewives can choose between
8 as many as six new regional shopping centres, whereas in the UK the choice at best is between the existing high street with its traffic fumes and lack of weather protection — and, frequently, lack of visual appeal — and a single modern centre. The latter must be ill-designed indeed if it cannot provide better facilities than the traditional high street. Quite apart from high standards of safety, convenience, cleanliness and comfort which undoubtedly appeal to the majority of shoppers, new centres are also able to provide off-street servicing to comply with modern standards of building and fire prevention, as well as improved car parking provision and schemes of integration with public transport.

Although shopping centre architecture in the past has not been of outstanding quality, talented architects,
19 far-sighted local authorities and sympathetic developers are capable of combining to produce buildings which will make a worth-while addition to our architectural heritage.

8 CHICAGO
Most shopping activity now takes place in suburban shopping centres, where the shopper has plenty of choice.

Note: Since this map was drawn, in 1971, more centres have been added to the Chicago area

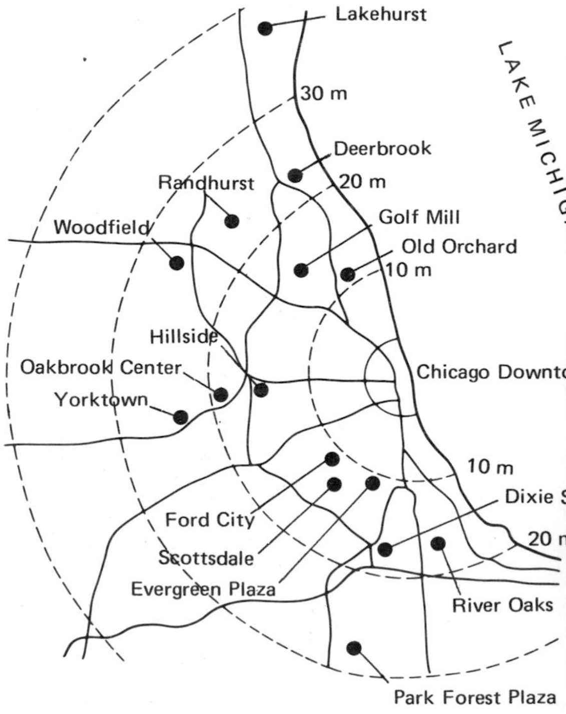

Express ways ______
Regional suburban shopping centres catchment population about 7 millions.
Total retail floor area in these 15 centres about 16 million ft^2.

ELDON SQUARE, NEWCASTLE UPON TYNE **9**

An interesting use of modern materials to integrate a new development with the architecture of an earlier period: the mirrored exterior of the shopping centre reflects the buildings opposite.

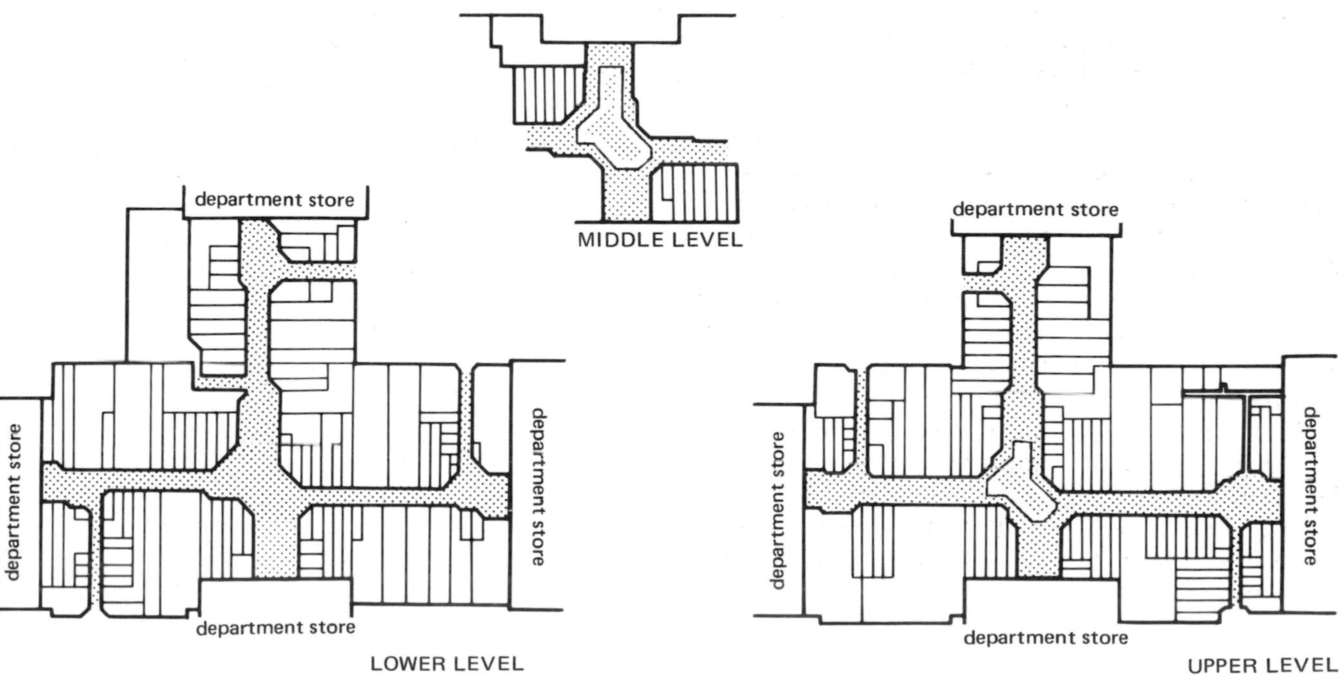

WOODFIELD MALL, CHICAGO **10**

A very large, multi-level, third generation, American out-of-town centre, with splayed frontages and nicely located entrances. Noteworthy also because of the use of half-levels across the malls, thereby reducing vertical travel.

Living with the traditional shopping street

The modern concept of a shopping centre probably originated in America where three factors created an opportunity for developing new comprehensive shopping facilities in the suburbs and on the peripheries of towns. These were:

- i The availability of large and cheap land areas in the suburbs
- ii An efficient and fast road network
- iii A high incidence of car ownership and a mobile affluent population.

At first sight these American centres bear little relationship to our shopping high street, but they do show one important characteristic essential to all successful shopping facilities: the generation of a
10 pedestrian flow which in turn induces sufficient trade to enable the retailer to trade profitably.

A glance at any of our busiest shopping streets (such
11 as Oxford Street and Brompton Road in London, Market Street in Manchester, Princes Street in Edinburgh and Northumberland Street in Newcastle) will confirm one common feature: the predominance of big traders, in particular the department stores such as House of Fraser, John Lewis Partnership and Debenhams, followed by chain stores such as Marks & Spencer, British Home Stores, C & A, Woolworths and Boots. It is the presence of these same retailers which will determine the strength of pedestrian movement in both a high street and a shopping centre. The trade of most retailers is directly proportional to the number of shoppers passing their shop windows, and the moment one moves to a location away from this peak flow, turnover falls dramatically. In this sense, therefore, the major shopping centre is simply a high street translated into modern terms with many important additional facilities such as adequate car parking, pedestrianisation, enclosure heating, cleanliness and off-street goods servicing.

The objective of the shopping centre developer is to provide the community with a modern, attractive and viable shopping facility in whatever setting may be available — high street, town centre or town perimeter. The form and design of the centre will be very much influenced by the nature of the site available. A town centre scheme may well have to compress into 10 acres or less the same facilities that would occupy 20 acres in a new town and 60 acres in an out-of-town scheme. It may also have to be integrated with existing buildings and take into account the preservation of old buildings. These factors all combine to make the town centre scheme more expensive to build than its out-of-town counterpart.

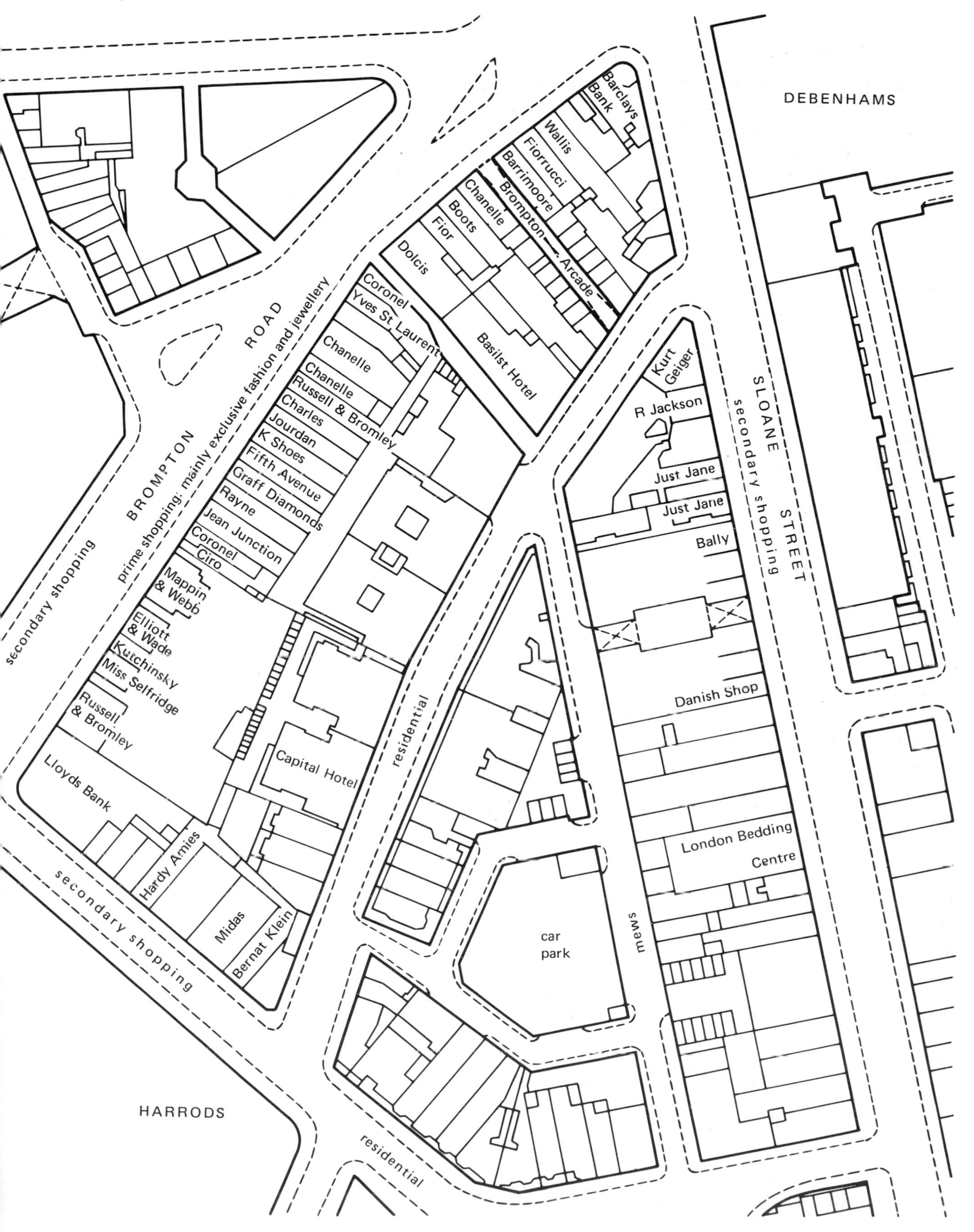

KNIGHTSBRIDGE, LONDON **11**

Because of its dense pedestrian flow, the shopping frontage to Brompton Road between Harrods and Sloane Street has one of the highest rental values in Britain. Note the high percentage of units occupied by multiple traders and chain stores. It is also worth noting that the other side of Brompton Road, separated from this frontage by a very busy road, has a materially lower trading density.

The relevance of overseas practice

The out-of-town or suburban shopping centre has developed rapidly in North America, Australia, Europe and elsewhere. In the UK the shortage of land and tight planning controls have limited the prospects for such
12 centres. Indeed, Brent Cross, which opened in the spring of 1976, is the first significant out-of-town shopping centre in the UK. In plan and concept it is very similar to many such centres developed overseas, and undoubtedly if any other out-of-town shopping centres were developed in suburban locations in the UK they would tend to be in the same form.

The fact that most of our larger shopping centres built in the UK in the past decade have been located in town centres has sometimes wrongly led to the conclusion that overseas experience is irrelevant to the problems of rebuilding our central areas. The physical solutions to many of the planning problems may vary tremendously, depending upon the nature and limitations of the site. Clearly a regional shopping centre occupying between 50 and 100 acres in North America will take a very different form if it is compressed into a site of 10 acres and possibly integrated with other developments such as offices, flats and recreational centres.

12 BRENT CROSS, NORTH LONDON
An out-of-town enclosed two-level regional shopping centre — a successful centre with a very high standard of internal finishes.

13 LE CARREFOUR LAVAL, MONTREAL
A large regional centre with 'magnet' department stores and a shop tenant mix planned to stimulate pedestrian flow. Note how the frontages to the shop units at points of peak pedestrian flow have been reduced to gain maximum representation at these points. Pascals and Simpsons, however, have unnecessarily long frontages to the malls which do result in a loss of visual interest at these points.

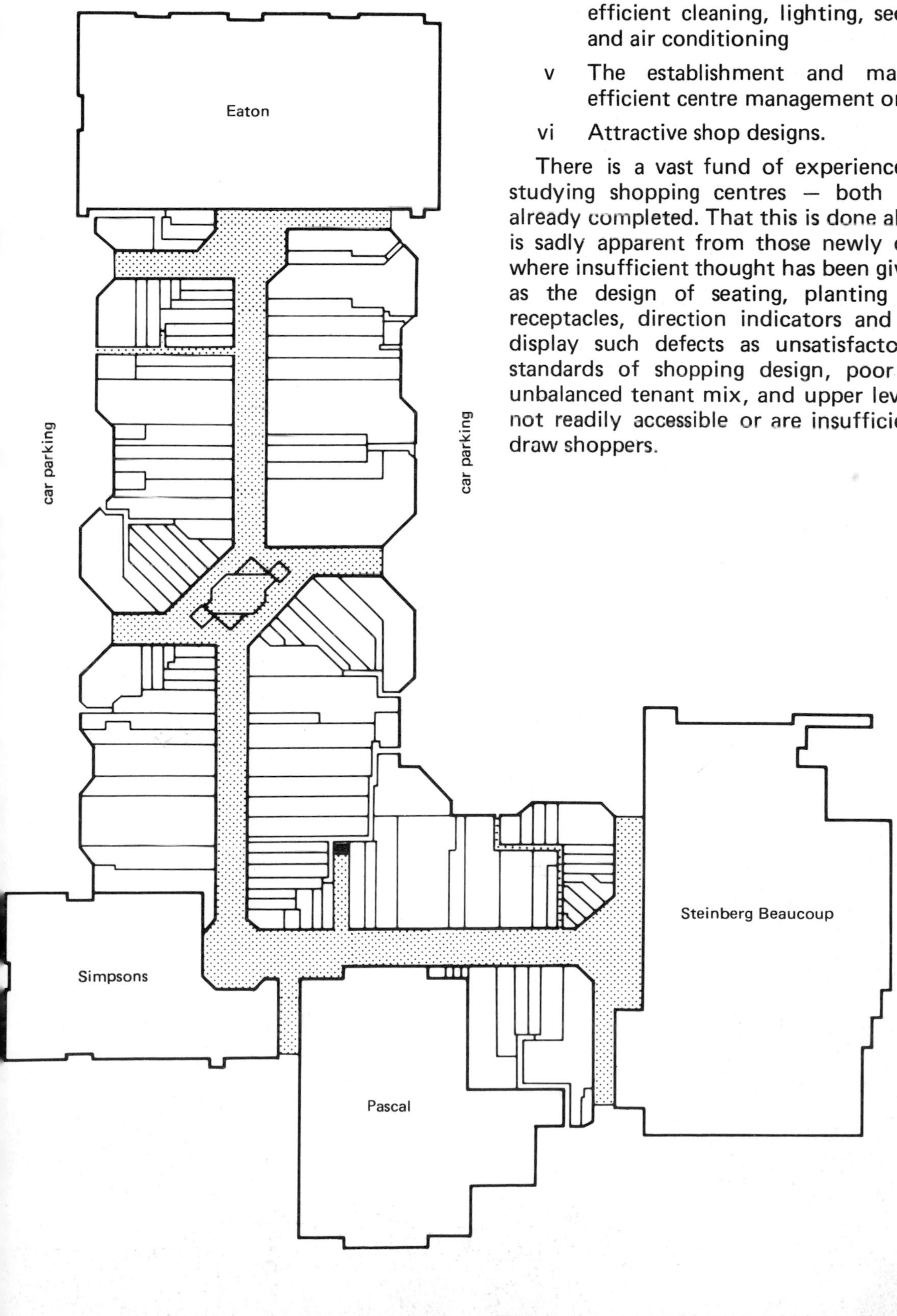

Eaton
car parking
car parking
Simpsons
Steinberg Beaucoup
Pascal

Nevertheless, all types of shopping centre, if they are correctly planned, have a number of features in common:

i An efficient pedestrian flow
ii A well-planned tenant mix 13
iii A design achieving an environment which is attractive to shoppers and efficient to manage 14
iv The use of appropriate building materials, techniques and detailing in order to achieve efficient cleaning, lighting, security, ventilation and air conditioning
v The establishment and maintenance of an efficient centre management organisation
vi Attractive shop designs.

There is a vast fund of experience to be found by studying shopping centres — both good and bad — already completed. That this is done all too infrequently is sadly apparent from those newly completed centres where insufficient thought has been given to such details
as the design of seating, planting features, rubbish 15
receptacles, direction indicators and signs, and which 16
display such defects as unsatisfactory flooring, poor standards of shopping design, poor pedestrian flow, unbalanced tenant mix, and upper level malls which are not readily accessible or are insufficiently attractive to draw shoppers.

14 *Enclosed centres can provide a high standard of decor which is attractive to shoppers:*

14a ROSNY 2, PARIS

14b YORKDALE, TORONTO

Rubbish receptacles: attractive appearance, careful siting and functional design are all-important: 15

EASTGATE MALL, HAMILTON, ONTARIO **15a**

SCARBOROUGH TOWN CENTRE, TORONTO **15b**

WOODFIELD MALL, CHICAGO **15c**

SCARBOROUGH TOWN CENTRE, TORONTO **16a**

ELDON SQUARE, NEWCASTLE UPON TYNE **16b**

LE CARREFOUR LAVAL, MONTREAL **16c**

WOODFIELD MALL, CHICAGO **16d**

Seating: this needs to be carefully integrated into the mall design: 16

Implications of enclosure

As previously explained, planning legislation in the United States has allowed the development of centres within short distances of each other; and the fast road network and the mobility of shoppers have resulted in very keen competition. It was found that schemes could be made measurably more attractive – and therefore commercially more successful – by covering them and thus creating a more pleasant environment: indeed, so
17 much so that a number of open centres have been covered, at considerable expense, and subsequent trading levels have justified the cost.

Effective planning control in the UK has tended to restrict the number of new centres to be built both in the town centres and in the suburbs. Competition between open and covered centres has therefore been much more restrained, and to date there has been no commercial benefit in enclosing open centres in order to maintain or recapture retail trade. Nevertheless, the high trading levels achieved in covered centres do indicate that the shopper appears to find them preferable to the typical high street or shopping precinct. Although it is not easy to quantify the commercial advantage of the covered centre over others, its prime virtue is that it provides an opportunity to create a controlled
18 environment with a character specially designed for the shopper. It can be vehicle-free – as indeed can any pedestrianised street – but it can also be cleaner, free from bad weather and more attractively designed. The shopkeeper can take advantage of this superior environment to open up his shop front to encourage the shopper into his unit, and can select his finishing materials from a much wider range which do not need to be weatherproof.

The aesthetic design of the covered areas is of great importance, for it will provide an overall special identity peculiar to the centre, not only attractive to the women shoppers, who expend most of the family money, but also reflecting the type of trading level the centre sets out to achieve. An Oxford Street shopper would feel at home in surroundings distinctly different from those which would attract, say, Burlington Arcade shoppers. The importance of the appeal to women shoppers must not be under-estimated in a successful centre, as they may represent 80% of all visitors.

In the UK, little or no attention seems to be paid to the wide range of opportunities which are available. Our centres are so similar as almost to have been produced on a conveyor belt. Certainly no attempt has been made to produce the differences of appearance which exist,
19 for example, between Place Ville Marie in Montreal, Woodfield Mall in Chicago, Eastgate Mall in Hamilton, 2001 McGill Metro in Montreal, and the Shop in Shop at Altona, Hamburg.

EGLINGTON SQUARE, TORONTO **17**
Built as an open centre but subsequently enclosed

Examples of a quality of environment possible only in an enclosed centre: **18**

VELIZY 2, PARIS **18a**

18b ROSNY 2, PARIS

BELLE EPINE, PARIS **18c**

A variety of design treatments: **19**

PLACE VILLE MARIE, TORONTO **19a**

Note the special treatment to cope with the low ceiling height. This extension area has been carefully detailed to the same high standard as the main shopping arcades, but with a different design theme.

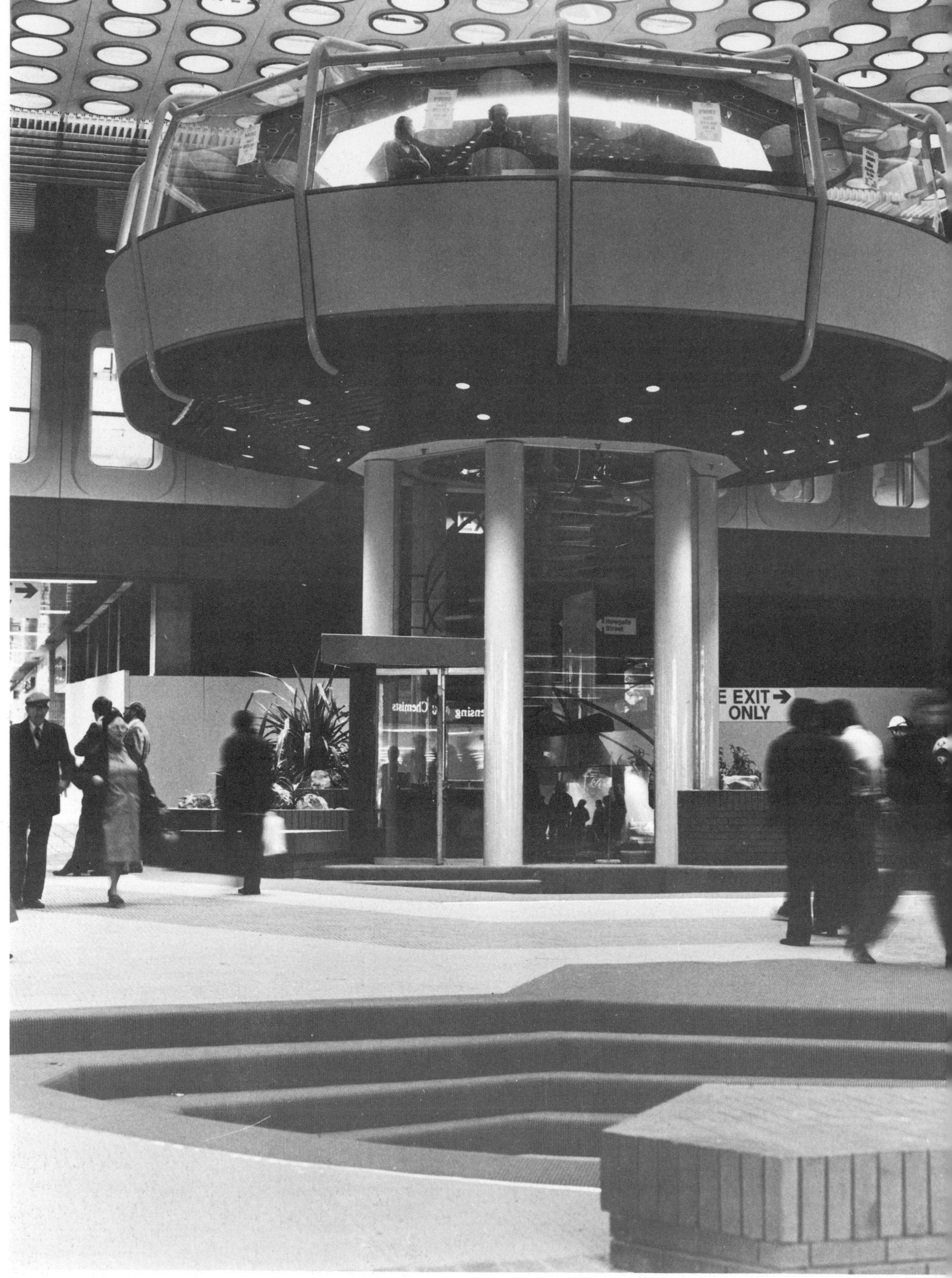

19b ELDON SQUARE, NEWCASTLE UPON TYNE
The coffee shop and seating well

SCARBOROUGH TOWN CENTRE, TORONTO **19c**

OLD ORCHARD, CHICAGO **20**

A highly successful open centre which is well planned and managed, and is thus able to compete with newer centres

The internal design need not consist merely of walls, floors and roof, decorated as they may be, with the shops simply units opening off some dominant hall. There is scope for a more subtle solution which provides an environment with special characteristics and appeal and a greater association between the shopper and the shopkeeper. Possibly because this is such a specialised problem, North American experience tends to the view that it is an area best dealt with by specialist designers and not treated simply as an extension of the basic architectural building design problems.

Enclosure will involve additional costs; requirements for the building volume will be larger; expensive decorative materials will be used; and the problems of fire control will need to be overcome. Fire control can result in compartmentation, dividing spaces which visually need to be uninterrupted; and it will almost certainly require ceiling barriers to contain smoke, which, if the ceilings are too low, will obstruct the views down the malls.

One particular problem arises as a result of a pleasant environment: it may attract hooligans and layabouts. Although more delicate materials can be selected with visual advantage, special care has to be taken with their detailing to overcome the problems of vandalism and high maintenance costs which can arise. Whilst local authorities will often prefer to see the malls kept open at nights, this is not usually feasible in practice because of the increased security risks and vulnerability to vandalism. In the design stage, provision should always be made for complete closure of the centre at night. The police cannot fully exercise their powers over private land, and some internal security system, probably involving patrols, will be necessary.

A smaller amount of rubbish is more noticeable in an otherwise clean environment, and special and more frequent arrangements are necessary to keep the centre clean.

Enclosure therefore involves a number of problems and much higher initial and running costs, but its advantages must not be overlooked, for it can provide a far greater degree of comfort and a more pleasant environment for the shopper, who has to be attracted if the centre is to be successful.

Design implications of open centres

The earlier examples of North American shopping
20 centres, such as the Old Orchard at Chicago, were of
course of the open type. No matter which type of centre is selected, the same principles of pedestrian flow with its careful disposition of 'magnet' traders and entrances should be adopted, and the main difference is one of environment.

The choice of finishing materials will be restricted in the case of an open centre, for they all have to be weatherproof and some means of protecting the shopper, such as canopies, needs to be provided. Care needs also to be taken to ensure that excessively windy conditions are avoided. Courtyard areas linked by short covered arcades can unexpectedly channel the wind, and taller buildings, by a vortex effect, can considerably speed up the wind. The building form and layout must therefore be studied to ensure that reasonable conditions will be provided. Fire precautions will be less stringent, for the shopping malls will be in the open and normally the Fire Brigade can readily obtain access to all parts of the complex. In the open areas, subtle colour changes will be less apparent, and flooring patterns, for example, need to be much bolder.

Whereas in a covered centre the shops and their merchandise can dominate, in the open centre, where they are protected by their weatherproof front, it is almost inevitably the public areas which become visually more important. A bolder approach to the detailing problems and colour schemes is therefore necessary if they are to tell, and a more robust character is required throughout.

It must be recognised that possibly for some years to come large new enclosed centres may not be viable. Local authorities will need to consider carefully more modest schemes of redevelopment, including the
pedestrianisation of existing streets and the 21
refurbishment of existing buildings — solutions which 22
are frequently achieved with considerable success. 23

KAUFINGERSTRASSE, MUNICH **21**
An example of a pedestrianised street

4 Fundamental principles of shopping centre planning

Identification of the need for new or additional retail facilities

Perhaps the first and most important step in establishing a new centre is to determine the need for new facilities. In the past, developers have been too ready to assume that the grant of planning consent implied a belief by the planning authority that a need existed for the amount of space approved. Equally, planners were apt to believe that developers would build a new shopping centre only if they were sure that sufficient retail demand existed to absorb the space provided. Since under the Community Land Act the local authority is almost certain to have an involvement with developments of any significance, it would seem appropriate for the authority either to undertake a retail demand survey or to require the developer to do this.

22 THE BROADWAY, BRADFORD
A pedestrianised street

Site assembly

Site assembly in a central area was one of the developer's greatest problems where he was not working in partnership with the local authority. In the future this may be less of a difficulty in the UK as the local authority will probably be initiating the development and will acquire the land required if it has not already done so. The size of the site area should receive early consideration and the date for vacant possession should be determined. Developers should not under-estimate the problems of site assembly, both within and outside the UK, in a town centre where the local authority is unwilling or unable to use powers of compulsory purchase to acquire land interests. There is a grave risk that the lion's share of the developer's profit will go to the least co-operative site owners, who will soon recognise the strength of their negotiating positions with a developer who is heavily committed to proceed with the development.

It may well be that in a central area redevelopment considerable site works will be needed, such as underpinning of adjoining owners' properties, demolition works, and re-routing of sewers, drains, electricity, gas and other services. Similarly, there may be road closures and the relocating of existing occupiers to be undertaken. Considerable work may be necessary, and possibly a network analysis will have to be undertaken to determine the earliest feasible date for site possession.

Determining the general character of the centre

Once the need for additional retail facilities has been established, the general form of development must be considered. Although work on detailed sketch plans should be delayed until much information has been accumulated, some thought needs to be given to such matters as the site area and location and its relationship with existing or proposed road patterns and bus services. It is essential to form a clear impression of the development concept at an early stage and to resolve basic ideas where this is possible, although it may be necessary to modify these later when viability studies have been undertaken.

Points which could usefully be considered at this stage include site access and means of servicing, names of key tenants, the inclusion of complementary uses such as offices, flats and bus stations, and physical and planning restrictions to the site.

Selecting key tenants

Successful shopping centres are designed around key tenants such as department stores, variety stores, specialist stores and supermarkets. Letting cannot be left to chance and discussions with key tenants should be initiated well before any detailed drawings are available. Letting negotiations with such tenants can be reckoned in terms of years rather than months, and the sooner a start is made, the better. It must be accepted that there will probably be at least one abortive negotiation for every key letting achieved.

If the development is a joint venture between a local authority and a commercial developer, it is almost certain that they will be entering into major commitment decisions long before a binding agreement can be reached with even the key tenants. Developers have all too frequently under-estimated the degree of risk which they are carrying at this stage. Local authorities must appreciate that they are relying on the developer's judgment of his ability to select the most suitable tenants and to achieve a letting on satisfactory terms.

When the development is complete, it will be the composition, character and strength of the tenants which will determine its commercial success. No amount of expenditure on building finishes can compensate for a weak selection of tenants or a bad tenant mix.

Relations with the local authority

A successful and efficiently run development will depend much on the establishment of a satisfactory relationship between the local authority and the developer. Both parties must be capable of seeing beyond their immediate requirement — in, say, negotiating a ground rent — and must look towards the setting up of a workable partnership which, apart from being equitable to all parties, will provide a firm foundation upon which to build a development team. It must be capable of coping with the sundry problems which will surely arise even in a successful development. Some of the objectives of the local authority and the developer, as well as of the funding institution if that is also involved, are bound to conflict.

There is much to be said for delaying the negotiation of the detailed terms of the building lease to the developer until full information — including sketch schemes, cost estimates, etc — is available and the developer is in a position to instruct his architect to prepare detailed drawings.

Relations with the local community

In the case of a large scheme it is as well to give some thought to public relations with the community. There are often many pressure groups which will oppose any new building works, and a wise developer will ensure that there are periodic press releases, interviews and possibly explanations to interested bodies, all of which help to keep the public properly informed as to the merits and progress of a development scheme.

On a major development scheme it may well be desirable to establish a public relations policy and programme which is likely to have varying objectives during the course of development. Initially it will be essential to see that the merits of the scheme are properly publicised. Community benefits such as pedestrianisation, off-street servicing, car parking, weather protection, cleanliness, leisure activities and new stores must be properly explained. Quite apart from improving community relations, this will assist in getting the centre known to the shopping public when it opens for trade.

Establishing the development team and centre management organisation

The selection of professional consultants is covered in Section 11. Nevertheless, some consideration should be given at the outset to the role of the local authority as a member of the development team, as well as to the possible involvement of the developer as the project manager. Creating an effective development team is not merely a case of briefing a number of consultants. Experience has shown that the team must be co-ordinated and led by an experienced project manager. If the developer has the in-house staff to do this, it is in his best interests to hold firmly on to the overall control of the project. However, if in-house staff are not available, great care must be taken in selecting the consultants, who may not necessarily have the same objectives as the client.

The appointment of the centre manager and his staff comes at a later stage, but consideration should be given to problems of property management before the design is too far advanced.

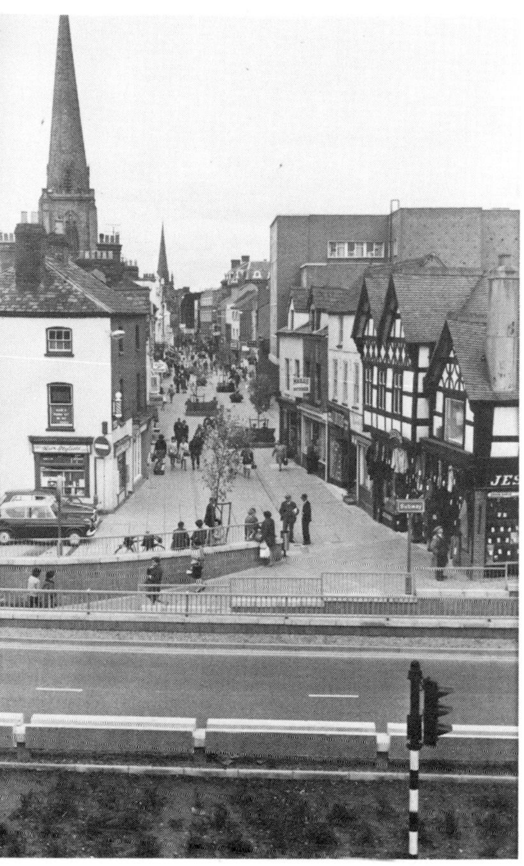

EIGN GATE, HEREFORD **23**
A subway under the ringroad leads to the pedestrianised shopping street.

If satisfactory solutions to the matters examined under the heading of basic principles appear to be forthcoming, then the developer may justifiably proceed to the next stage and work towards detailed viability studies based on preliminary sketch layouts. The detailed sequence of operations is explained in Section 12.

Transport, parking and access facilities

The size of the shopping catchment area and therefore the trading potential of a centre will depend on the standard of transport and parking facilities available to the shopper. For the car shopper, time may be more critical than distance and the proximity of a motorway could be of vital importance. Access roads to the centre, which may be outside the control of the developer, must be able to take the extra flow of traffic created by the centre.

Similarly, in many UK centres the public transport system is of crucial importance and is likely to remain so for the foreseeable future. Bus stops ought to be located to bring shoppers right into the centre.

Development finance

A few years ago the provision of development finance was not a major obstacle to development. Developers were usually content to enter into a firm development commitment in the knowledge that short term bridging finance would be readily available with minimal, if any, security where a developer had a reasonable track record. Permanent finance, usually by way of a sale and lease-back or an outright sale, was then arranged at the end of the development when success was assured and the financial terms were more favourable to the developer. The experience of the property slump in 1974/5 has now completely changed the funding climate, and the following conditions now exist:

- i The clearing banks will no longer lend large sums for property development unless very adequate security is available
- ii Bank lending interest rates are at least 2-3% above the bank base rate (14% November 1976)
- iii Building costs are rising more quickly than rental levels, which are fairly stable, and it is therefore exceptionally difficult to create a viable development
- iv The principal funding institutions such as pension and insurance funds are particularly reluctant to lend money for development projects unless they are small.

The lesson to be learned from this experience is that although most developers will readily undertake a measure of risk, they are most unlikely, at least for some time to come, to take on a major development commitment unless the long term development finance has been secured beforehand.

5 Siting the centre

Urban areas

Integrating with existing property

There are probably no problems which exercise the shopping centre team to a greater extent than those involved with planning in city centre or down-town locations – difficulties of piecing together different plots of land, dealing with the inevitable pressures from preservation groups, coping with the concern of the existing shopkeepers as to the effect that the centre will have on their trading, and overcoming the problems of building on a congested site; and there is also the difficulty of finding a plan solution which resolves the basic layout problems on a site which will almost certainly be severely limited in size and shape.

It is essential that the existing and potential shopper
24 flows from the surrounding areas are evaluated as early as possible. These flows might be from an existing shopping area, from a nearby department store, from bus stops or stations, from existing car park areas, or from adjacent residential or office areas – or, if the developer is lucky, from some public right of way crossing the site. Once these flows have been recognised, then the major new elements in the centre need to be located to capture, increase and extend them.

City centre sites are often so valuable that to make the best use of space multi-level solutions are essential. The shopping centre team will find that the ability to recognise some subtle change in ground level sufficient to provide an entrance into a different mall level at the correct point, and to manipulate a cramped space to provide a special interchange of levels, are real skills to be treasured.

The final arrangement, even on a congested site, must provide a simple layout with concentrated pedestrian flow through all parts of the centre. The shoppers have to be guided directly into the different parts without realising that they have been given no choice of route, for success cannot be guaranteed and is indeed unlikely if in a multi-level centre all the entrances are at one level and the shoppers are expected to change level within the centre.

Basic design principles must still be adopted even within the severe constraints which undoubtedly exist in down-town locations. Special care should also be taken with regard to the atmosphere created by the appearance and design of the centre. A super-de-luxe centre may not be welcomed, for example, by the citizens of Windsor; on the other hand, an olde-worlde character would not really be suitable in the centre of Newcastle.

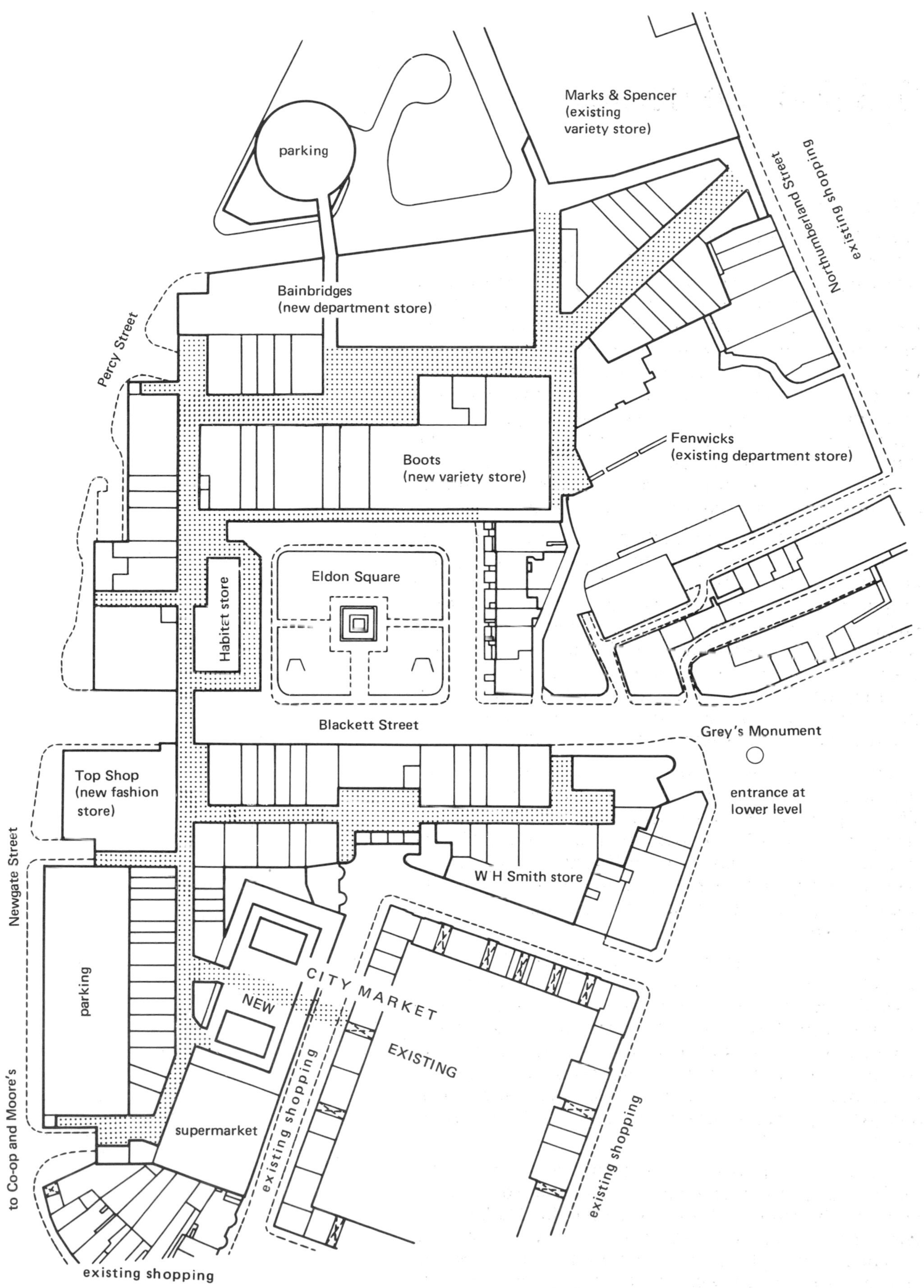

ELDON SQUARE, NEWCASTLE UPON TYNE **24**

This downtown centre links several shopping areas in the centre of Newcastle. In spite of severe limitations arising from the shape of the development, anchor traders have been located to stimulate pedestrian flow.

Problems of townscape

Down-town locations invariably involve problems of preservation of existing buildings and integration of the new with the old.

In times of economic growth there is rarely any real commercial advantage in retaining existing buildings, for they will invariably place some severe limitation on the planning of the buildings behind. However, very often there are buildings with historical links or of architectural importance which have to be preserved, and great care is necessary in evaluating the problems arising from the retention of these buildings. The effect on the planning of the centre needs to be weighed, and the question whether an entire building needs to be retained or whether the facade is sufficient must be considered.

25 The cost can be high. For example, the Nelson Street facade at Eldon Square, which it was very worth-while retaining, cost (in 1974-5) some £150 000, or something in the order of £2 200 for each metre of its length. In this case the varying levels of fenestration required a separate new building behind the old facade.

Sometimes (although rarely) the site will be clear and unencumbered by planning restrictions regarding heights and materials, but it still remains important that new buildings integrate well with their surroundings, and care is necessary with regard to the scale, detailing and choice of finishing materials. There can be no hard and fast rules for this type of problem, and the developer is almost completely in the hands of his designer and the planning authority.

25 NELSON STREET, NEWCASTLE UPON TYNE
A preserved Georgian facade which has been meticulously incorporated into the Eldon Square development.

Clayton Street before development **26a**

Clayton Street after development **26b**

Quite apart from the problems of integrating new architecture with old, it sometimes happens that an existing street becomes the rear access to a shop fronting an enclosed mall. This introduces special problems for the architect, who will need to use all his design skills to create an exciting elevation from the back of a shop. It can be done, as will be seen from the
26 illustration of Clayton Street, Newcastle upon Tyne, before and after development.

Out of town areas

The opportunities for experimenting with design in planning developments in town centres are usually very limited and the developer's main concern is to find a workable solution within the confines of the existing setting. In a suburban location with a greater land availability, however, the architect has considerable freedom to achieve a more efficient and more economical solution. Often car parks and peripheral goods servicing areas are far cheaper to construct and maintain than covered car parks and service roads which have to be lit, ventilated and provided with sprinklers. However, in spite of its initial economy, open car parking is expensive in land and can present a most unsightly appearance, in addition to isolating the shopping centre from adjacent communal activities.

Whilst the opportunities for new suburban shopping in the UK must be very limited, there may well be opportunities in new and expanding towns to take advantage of the suburban or out-of-town shopping concept. Although the new town concept was first developed in this country, the shopping centres which form the heart of the new town communities have, without exception, lagged behind the best and latest thinking and design techniques. All too often there has been a gap in our understanding of what the housewife or the shopper really wants and what the architect believes she should have. The problem is no doubt aggravated by the fact that the shopper rarely has any opportunity to express her opinion before a centre is open and trading.

Very often the opportunities for suburban shopping centres will be for district and neighbourhood centres anchored at best on a small department store and at least on a food supermarket. Whilst the same pedestrian flow principles will apply, the restricted level of rentals and therefore the budget available will probably be a limiting factor in both the planning and the standard of finishes which can be applied.

27 GHIRARDELLI SQUARE, SAN FRANCISCO

27a *A section drawing illustrating how, with ingenuity, a group of existing buildings can be adapted, refurbished and given a new lease of life as a modern and attractive shopping complex.*

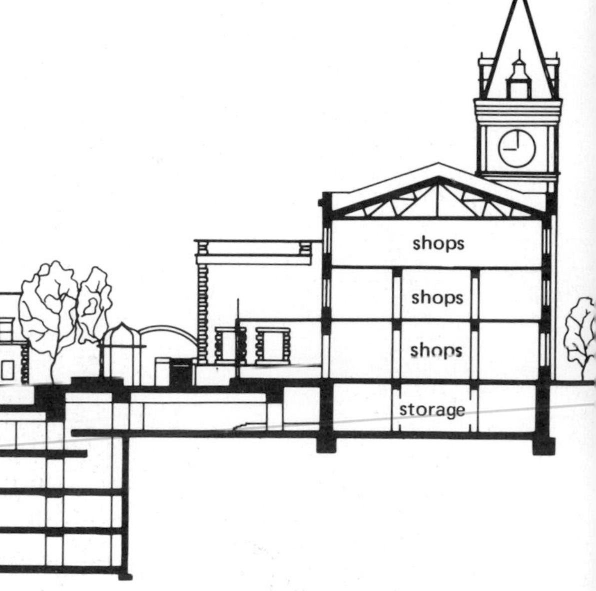

restaurant

arcade

shops

parking

GHIRARDELLI SQUARE **27b**
The Clock Tower

Schemes of refurbishment and pedestrianisation

Opportunities for major comprehensive central area redevelopments are likely to be very limited for the next few years, and local authorities and development companies will be obliged to consider less ambitious plans, including refurbishment and pedestrianisation. *27*
Although such schemes may not provide the shopping facilities for either shopper or retailer which can be available in a shopping centre, they can nevertheless provide shops which are convenient, safe from vehicular traffic and attractive in terms of street architecture. Where the existing street contains buildings worthy of preservation, redevelopment may be out of the question. In such cases the local authority may think it desirable to establish a tenant mix policy and to produce a positive detailed policy to control standards of shop front design. It is remarkable how many well known national multiple chains persuade themselves that poorly designed shop fascias and lettering should remain unchanged in case their national image is upset. It is equally astonishing to the non-retailer that an improvement in shop design can so significantly increase the retailer's turnover.

To date there has been little attempt to analyse and examine the problems of refurbished shopping areas but the basic shopping layout, tenant mix and pedestrian flow philosophies can still be used to advantage. To be really successful, however, it will be necessary to hunt out and examine the best international solutions and then apply the lessons learned. If this is not done, as with the covered centre, costly mistakes will be made and bitter and expensive experiences will be suffered. Successful solutions result only if the philosophy is understood, and it is courting disaster simply to tackle the problem without research in depth and a real appreciation of the complex retailing and development problems involved.

GHIRARDELLI SQUARE **27c**
A general view

6 Fundamental principles of shopping centre design

The key to a successful shopping centre plan is undoubtedly a concentrated pedestrian flow pattern. Its importance cannot be over-stressed, for it is self-evident that successful shopping streets are those along which most shoppers pass. It is the concentration of shoppers which attracts the shops, and the greater the concentration the better the shops that will be attracted. The ideal shopping centre plan will encourage high pedestrian flow through all its parts, producing not only the maximum rent potential, but also the busy, lively atmosphere a successful centre must have.

The basic principle in achieving this is to balance those parts of the centre which most shoppers will wish to visit, ie the 'magnets', in such a way that they will easily and readily pass through other parts in order to get there. The key factors are the location of the points of entry — be they from streets, large car parking areas, bus stations or some other point — and the disposition of important traders. They should be so arranged as to encourage the maximum flow of shoppers between them.

There are often pressures from designers and planners
28 to provide a variety of routes, normally with the intention both of giving shoppers an opportunity to meander and of creating areas of different interest: although, rather strangely, these same designers often impose some strong repetitive architectural theme which defeats this object. However, this type of plan has to be discouraged, for it has the strong disadvantage that it dilutes the pedestrian flow. Some routes become stronger than others and so some shops capture more trade than others and overall retail potential and balance is lost.

It is important, however, that the layout is kept simple. It is seldom appreciated how tiring the shopping expedition is, and this consideration effectively limits the physical size of the centre, as well as calling for the provision of some resting spots. Experience has shown that there is a maximum distance of about 200-250 metres (600-800 ft) which shoppers are prepared to travel from one major focal point to another. If distances are greater than this, they tend to lose interest and fail to complete the journey. If the pedestrian flow is to be uniform, it is desirable for the shopper to be physically capable of visiting all parts of the centre on one trip, and this is unlikely if the distances become too great.

28 ROOSEVELT FIELDS, LONG ISLAND
Opened in 1956, this was one of the first generation of American out-of-town shopping centres. It was uncovered and had a complex plan which would not now be repeated.

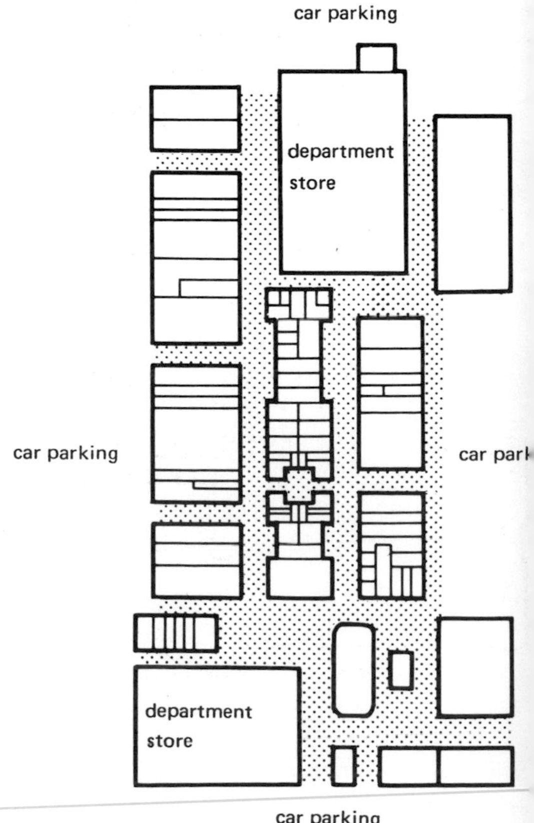

LE CARREFOUR LAVAL, MONTREAL **29**
This plan indicates how the service trades have been planned in locations of least importance. At first glance, their positions at the entrances would seem to be prestigious, but it should be remembered that there are seven entrances, so each has only about 15% of the potential pedestrian flow. The 'action' is in the malls, where peak trading density is achieved.

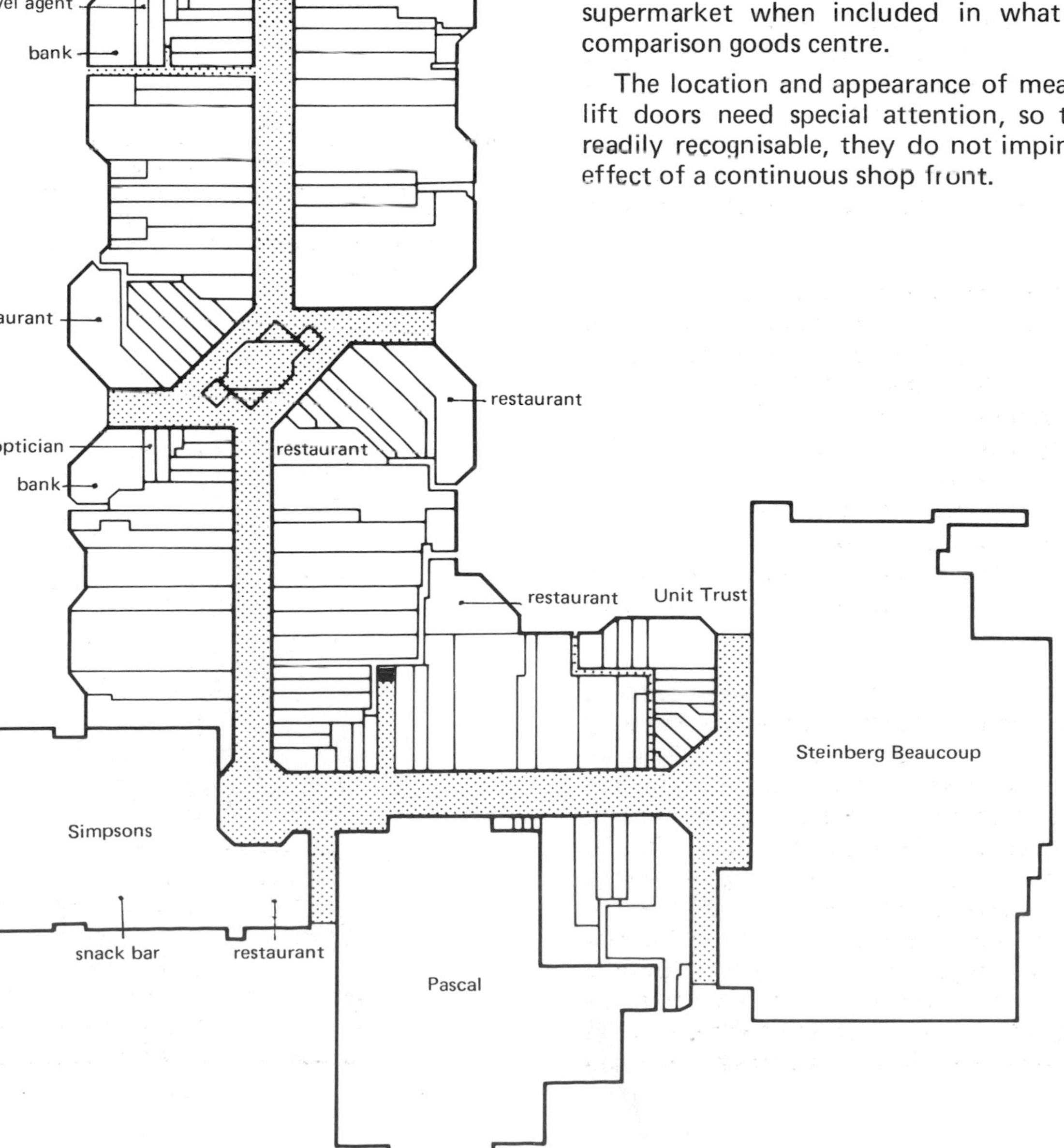

The adoption of what is called a tenant mix policy by carefully grouping and distributing the tenants according to their trades will further increase pedestrian flow. The old 'high street' philosophy of letting on a supply and demand basis has no place in a well-organised centre. This is not to say that competition is undesirable, for clearly it is to be welcomed: but excessive competition will defeat its own purpose. Skilful location and strict control of type and quality of tenant enable the organisation of competition so as actually to increase the pedestrian flow.

Once having settled the basic arrangement, it is then necessary to ensure that the shopper's interest is captured and kept. Shoppers basically come to shop; they will lose interest in areas where no merchandise is displayed, and the adjacent traders will suffer. For *29*
example, blank wall surfaces on the shop front line, even when carefully decorated, should be avoided, and the traditional bank or insurance company's front has no place in the main body of the mall. They are best located at some point on the periphery, and so is a food supermarket when included in what is principally a comparison goods centre.

The location and appearance of means of escape and lift doors need special attention, so that whilst being readily recognisable, they do not impinge on the overall effect of a continuous shop front.

The choice of location, shape and size of entrances needs particular care, for not only must they be in keeping with the scale of the building and physically large enough to accommodate the shoppers expected, but they should also be narrow enough to heighten the 'drama' of the main body of the centre when it is reached, and yet not so narrow as to cause unpleasant wind tunnel effects, which can easily occur even in covered centres.

The need to capture and keep shoppers' interest can lead to rather subtle problems. Ideally, once within the centre they should be walking towards some major attraction — a department store or a special central court, for example — rather than towards an entrance (though this is unavoidable if the entrance has been planned on a major axis). An outside view will almost inevitably dominate and the shopper could unwittingly and unexpectedly find herself outside the centre, when a deliberate decision would be required — and probably not taken — to turn round and re-enter. The best
30 entrances are those which attract shoppers into the centre, yet, whilst being readily recognisable, need a conscious effort to locate when the shopper is ready to leave.

30 VICTORIA CENTRE, NOTTINGHAM
The entrance from Lower Parliament Street used by pedestrian shoppers from the city centre.

Whilst the basic plan of the centre is being considered, the goods delivery arrangements must not be forgotten. It is undoubtedly simplest to provide vehicle space at the rear of each store and shop, but this can prove expensive in land cost and appear unsightly from the surrounding areas.

Particularly in central area locations, there are difficult and congested conditions for traders to overcome, and strictly from a commercial point of view, there is no measurable profit to be made from service areas. However, inefficient arrangements involve traders in heavy additional labour costs. What is required is the simplest, most direct method compatible with the land and building costs involved. Although all major stores and traders must have, and indeed will demand, specially allocated off-loading areas, other shops can use communal areas, hoists and corridors to deliver their goods; and it is well to remember that although there are undoubtedly peak delivery times, the number of off-loading bays can be reduced by taking advantage of the fact that different shops have different servicing requirements.

Where service facilities are severely restricted, then it may be necessary to resort to night deliveries; although if daily access can be provided, as at the Victoria Centre, Nottingham, it has been found there is little or no call for such arrangements.

An under-provision of goods servicing areas will make a Centre Manager's life very difficult, but an over-provision is a costly waste of resources. In the UK, compact central area schemes are invariably obliged to over-provide because of the need to use an enclosed service road.

One arrangement which involves quite heavy management costs and some security risk, but is certainly applicable when space is at a premium, is the provision of a manned receiving dock to which goods are delivered and from which they are collected at their convenience by the shop tenants, such as at Alexis Nihon, Toronto.

Once the basic overall dispositions have been decided, it is then necessary to consider in more detail the general shop areas. At this stage it is as well to bear in mind that to create a commercially successful centre it is desirable to achieve the maximum trading representation possible, and that there is therefore a premium on shop frontage. Shopkeepers need to be discouraged from taking more space than they really need and persuaded to utilise shopping frontages to the best advantage.

Too often, shops are laid out in an unimaginative and stereotyped pattern, the result being a number of units of similar area, depth and frontage which in turn result in an equally stereotyped structural grid. This approach does not recognise that different traders have different space needs, that higher overall rentals can be achieved if there is an inbuilt flexibility to accommodate different frontage widths, and that there is often considerable advantage to be gained by splaying frontages to encourage pedestrian flow and (used with discretion) foreshorten a perspective view and enliven a long row of shop units.

Whenever possible, advantage should be taken to incorporate 'T' and 'L' shaped units which, whilst providing tenants who require more space with adequate frontage representation, maximise the less valuable rear
31 area behind the smaller units. It is particularly important to ensure that the larger space users, who pay less than average rents per square foot, take minimum frontage and maximum rear space. Ideally the department store should have a wide entrance and no display frontage, which is expensive to fit out and has little influence on their trading turnover.

In principle, and consistent with cost, the structural grid should be made as large as possible. One in the order of 11 metres (36 ft) has much to commend it, for it will allow three 3.7 metre (12 ft) units, two 5.5 metre (18 ft) units, or one 3.7 metre and one 7.3 metre (24 ft) unit, all column free.

There is undoubtedly a tendency for shopkeepers to think primarily in terms of a regular-shaped plan, but
32 internationally it can be shown that splayed frontages need not reduce their trading level and that high turnovers can be achieved in irregular-shaped smaller units if the pedestrian flow potential is there.

It is worth remembering that different types of traders really need different shaped units. For example, a jeweller normally occupies a small unit, but he needs extensive window frontage to display his goods; on the other hand a shoe shop occupying a much larger area can trade effectively in a deep, relatively narrow unit.

A further point which should not be forgotten is that different traders require different storage facilities. The jeweller, for instance, needs very little, for nearly all his goods are on display, as is the case with most fashion shops. The shoe shop must, of course, have its storage close to the selling area, but for a trader who periodically re-stocks his shelves — say, a stationer or chemist — immediately adjacent storage areas are not really essential. The basic planning principle should be to arrange the shops within a flexible structural system in such a way as to straddle and guide the pedestrian flow past as many retailers as possible.

When considering the fundamental principles of planning a shopping centre, it is as well to bear in mind that a successful centre will probably lead to the need for expansion, and wherever possible some provision should be made for this in the future.

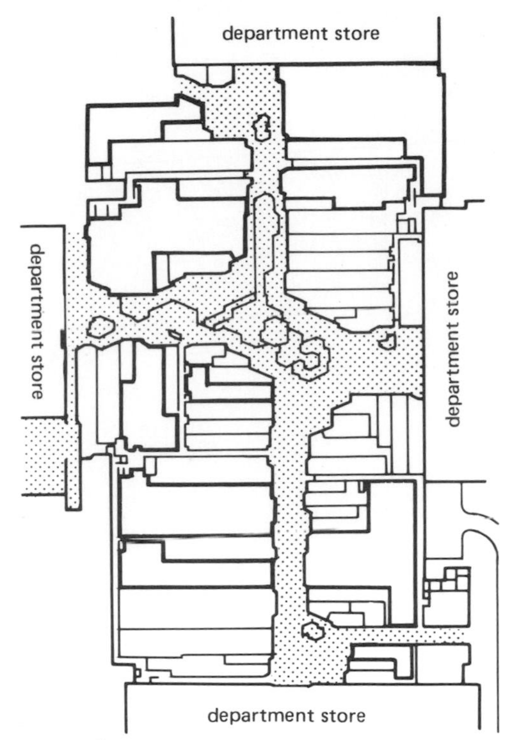

31 EASTRIDGE SHOPPING CENTRE, SAN JOSE, CALIFORNIA
This centre makes use of T-shaped and L-shaped units to maximise the rear space and to allow a greater number of traders within the same frontage length.

32 SCARBOROUGH TOWN CENTRE, TORONTO — upper level
This plan illustrates how the small, irregular-shaped units have been fitted together at key frontages, thereby increasing the number of tenants represented. Good designers will make use of the unusual shapes and provide exciting, attractive units — which anyway have the advantage of high trading potential.

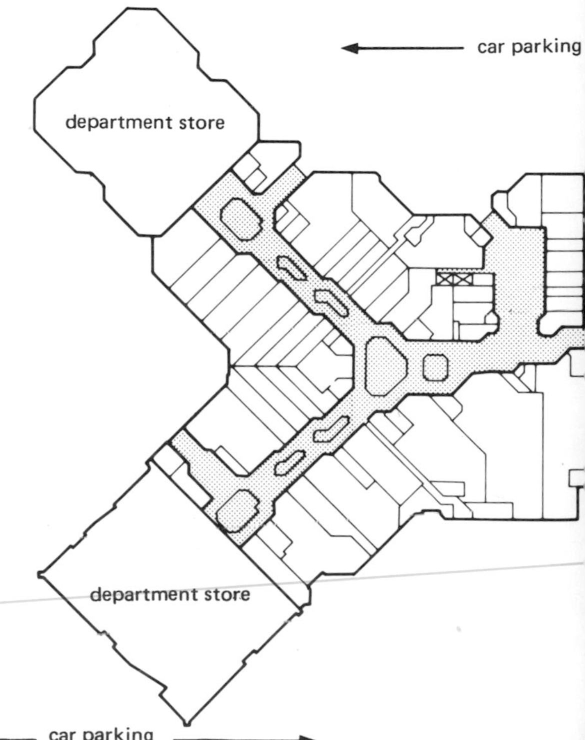

Clearly, large space users have widely differing requirements. In shape and disposition over three or more floors they can be surprisingly flexible. In a regional shopping centre some of our better known traders will have the following requirements:[1]

	Gross Internal Area Min		Max
John Lewis Partnership	150 000	to	250 000
Debenhams	100 000	to	150 000
Marks & Spencer	80 000	to	150 000
Boots Pure Drug Co. Ltd.	60 000	to	80 000
British Home Stores	60 000	to	80 000
Sainsbury	30 000	to	50 000
Waitrose	20 000	to	30 000
Miss Selfridge	8 000	to	12 000
Chelsea Girl	6 000	to	10 000
Habitat	12 000	to	16 000
W.H. Smith	20 000	to	25 000
Mothercare	6 000	to	10 000

The occupiers of standard units usually have more precise requirements; the following are given as a typical selection:

Name	*Trade*	*Frontage ft*	*Depth ft*	*Storage ft²*	*Total Area ft²*	*Remarks*
UDS Group						
Richard Shops	Ladies' fashion	27	100	300	3 500	
Collier	Male tailor	27	80	300	2 500	
Timpson Shoes	Shoes	27	80	300	2 500	
Suede Centre	Leatherwear	18	40	250	1 000	
Timpson Shoe Repairs	Shoe repairs	14	30	150	600	
Burton Group						
Superstore					15 000 – 20 000	'Good frontage required'
Burtons & Top Shop	Men's wear Ladies' fashion	30	–	1 500 – 2 000	3 000 – 5 000	Corner Sites still preferred
Green's Cameras	Camera, Hi Fi			500	1 500	No particular emphasis on depth or frontage
Evans Outsize	Outsize ladies' wear			500	1 500 – 1 700	
H Samuel	Jeweller	Corner site	100	1 000	2 sales floors 5 000 ft² + storage	
H Fenton	Male fashion	25	70	300	1 800 storage at different levels	
British Shoe Corporation						
Saxone, Dolcis, etc	Shoes	24	80–100	800	3 200	
Conleys	Jeweller	20	50	250	1 250	
Dorothy Perkins	Ladies' fashion	25	100	500	5 000	Stock/staff rooms at different level

1 The authors have drawn these figures solely from their own sources. They have not had access to any of the detailed information being collected as part of a CALUS Research study of retailers' requirements which was still in progress at the time that this publication was prepared.

7 Internal design

The mall

Dimensions and shape

Shopping malls need to be in the order of 13-15 metres (40-50 ft) and arcades 5-6 metres (15-20 ft) in width, the governing principle being that while a minimum clearance area of about 3 metres is needed to permit shoppers to perambulate, the shops on either side of the mall or arcade should not be so distant as to discourage crossing from one to the other.

Current advanced design thinking sometimes does not take into account the importance of the width of the mall. The analysis of the problem was one of the first lessons the North Americans learned, but with the development of the shopping centre theory and the search for new solutions, it is not always appreciated, or is perhaps forgotten, that the areas provided for the shopping public must be sufficient for the peak trading time densities. The central space in the mall will not only be available for seating, planting, litter bins and similar features, but will also provide an overflow space to reduce congestion. If the shops are to trade to their maximum potential, then the public areas must be adequate to meet the load. The decision whether arcades or malls are to be provided must carefully take into account not only the normal traffic of shoppers but also the numbers that will be present when the centre is busy.

As explained before, the malls should be simple in configuration and not more than about 200 metres (600 ft) long.

If the number of shops required cannot be planned astride a basically straight mall, then some special plan form needs to be adopted which must still provide a simple direct layout. Examples are off-centre malls, such
33 as the Esplanade Oxnard, California, the L-shaped mall with 'magnet' stores at the corner and at each end such as Yorkdale, Toronto, the doughnut arrangement such as Square 1, Montreal, and Exton Square, Pennsylvania, and the figure-of-8 such as the completed centre at Sherway Gardens, Toronto, will have. These solutions are all in principle based on a readily appreciated and simple plan form.

There is of course the further alternative of the multi-level solution, which will be inevitable where land costs are relatively high or where a single level mall would be excessive in length.

33 *A variety of mall shapes:*

department store
shops
shops
shops
shops
department store

33a ESPLANADE OXNARD, CALIFORNIA
A simple plan form with the major 'magnet' stores at either end of a long, straight mall. However, the mall has been arranged so that its two halves are off-centre when they meet at the centre court. Note how the entrances to this court are also off-centre, and how the entrances by the stores could be criticised because they are not.

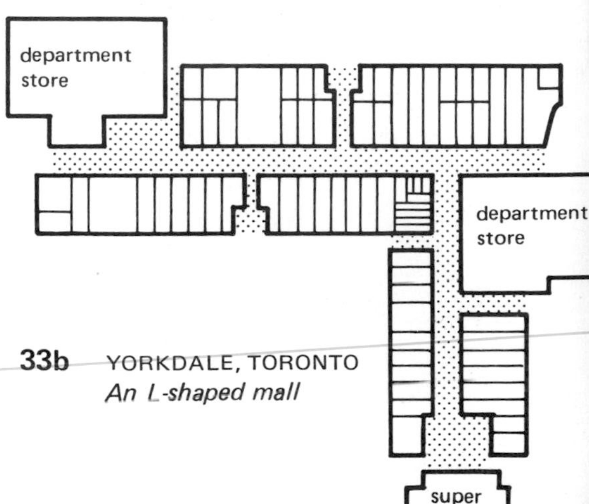

33b YORKDALE, TORONTO
An L-shaped mall

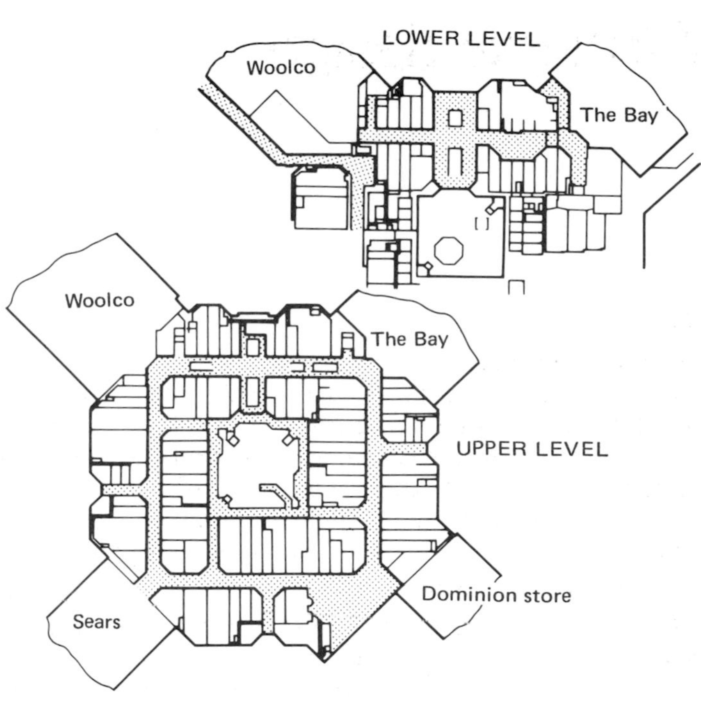

SQUARE ONE, MONTREAL **33c**
A square mall plan with anchor traders at each corner

EXTON SQUARE, PENNSYLVANIA **33d**
A square mall with a central anchor trader

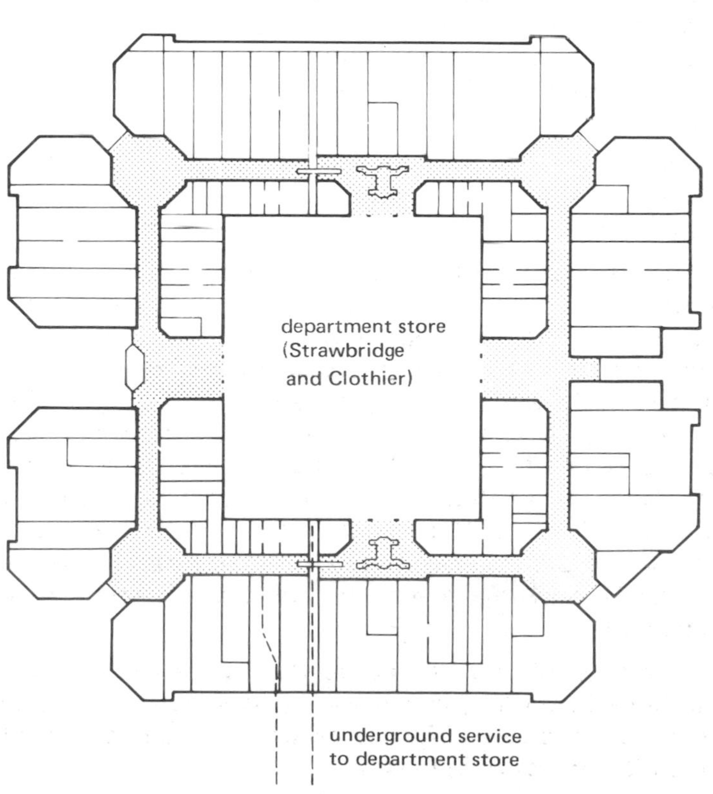

SHERWAY GARDENS, TORONTO **33e**
A figure-of-8 mall design. The plan illustrates the centre as it will be when the final phase is completed.

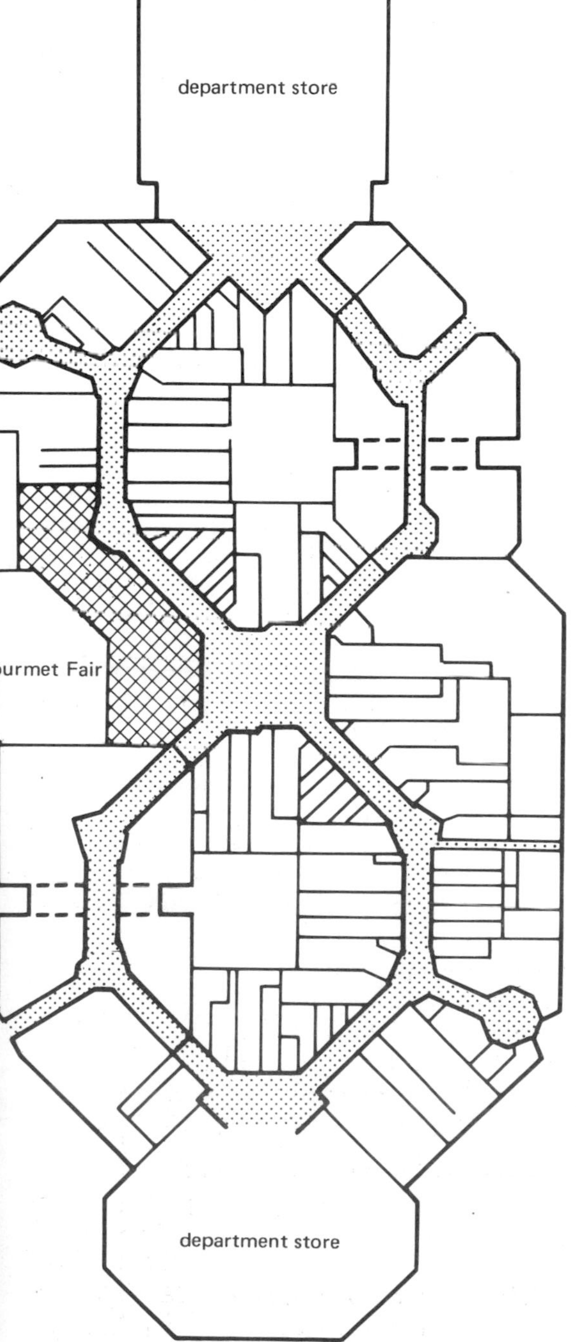

A potential area of development sadly little explored in this country is the use of splayed frontage lines. It has been noted that in North America many centres, for example Sherway Gardens, Toronto, and Woodfield Mall, Chicago, have successfully used this device at entrances and corners to control the pedestrian flow and subtly guide the shoppers past the shops, while at the same time creating spaces flowing from one to another.

A difficult problem with the simple straight mall layout can be the long, imposing perspective which results, giving rise to the 'visual stop' theory. Basically this concludes that 'if the shopper is not trapped she will pass through'. In other words, having achieved a concentrated pedestrian flow it is no good allowing the shoppers to be swept along with the tide: the run must be slowed down to encourage them to look into the shops they are passing. And so the proportions of the mall section and length, and what shoppers can see, become more critical.

For example, if the ceiling is raised, the mall space can overpower the shops; if it is lowered, the perspective increases. Some way needs to be found to foreshorten the distant view and yet at the same time guide the shopper from area to area. Splaying the shop fronts
34 down the malls, as has been done at Franklin Park Mall, Toledo, Ohio, can help in this problem: but discretion must be used, for unless great care is taken, some shop fronts can be blanketed and find themselves off the concentrated pedestrian flow lines.

Other solutions can be found in the subtly cranked malls at Scarborough Town, Toronto, or in placing the
35 malls slightly off-centre such as at Eastridge San Jose,
36 California. At the Victoria Centre, Nottingham, columns, stairs and lift shafts have been included in the mall central pausing areas. It has to be admitted that while this latter solution ensures that a centre never looks empty, even early in the day when few shoppers are present, it does lay itself open to the criticism that if the centre is highly successful, the barriers cause an impediment to the pedestrian flow. If the centre is not successful, these barriers will be criticised because the shops are not all immediately visible.

On the other hand, there are several examples of large centres well located in provincial towns and with many comparable 'magnet' qualities, but apparently not trading so well, at least partly because the malls are not visually stopped and potential shoppers pass through too quickly.

With regard to the height of the mall, it needs to be appreciated that a shop front height of less than 3.5 metres (11 ft) will considerably restrict the very desirable variations in shop front designs and will almost inevitably lead in the main to the traditional standard High Street fascia solution. A desirable clear mall height is therefore in the order of 4.5 metres (14 ft).

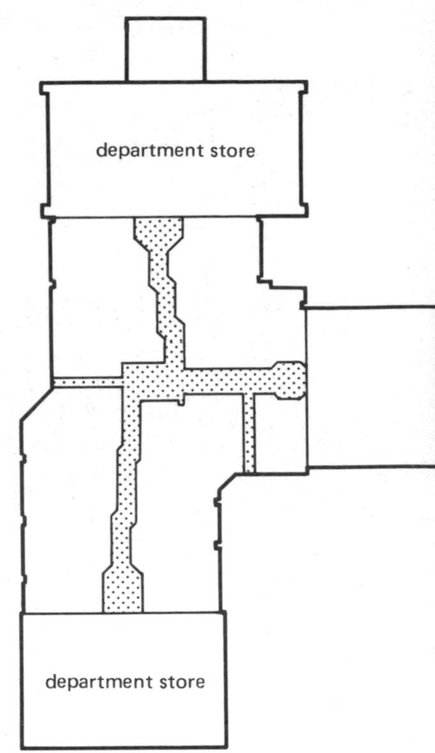

34 FRANKLIN PARK MALL, TOLEDO, OHIO
The splayed frontages are a device to add interest to otherwise straight malls.

35 SCARBOROUGH TOWN CENTRE, TORONTO – lower level
The subtly cranked malls, which guide shoppers along and always provide something of interest to look at, have been achieved by splaying the shop fronts. Note how the entrances (and exits) have been planned away from the main axes.

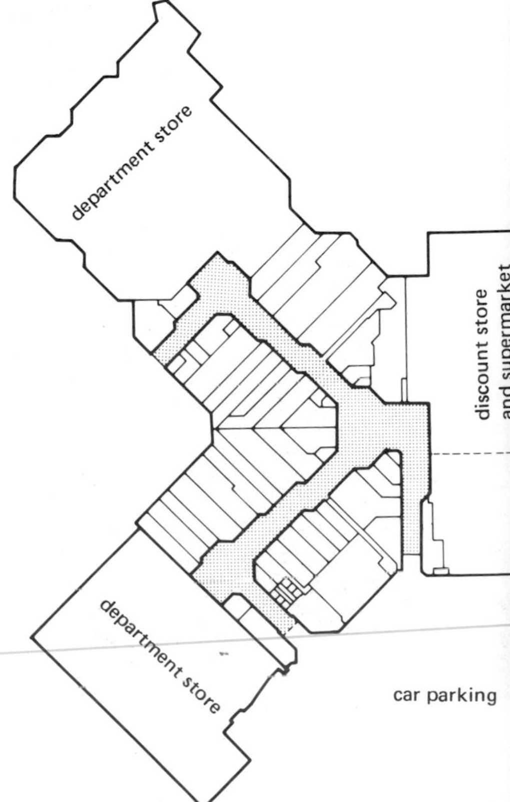

VICTORIA CENTRE, NOTTINGHAM **36**

The central staircase and lift shaft break up an unduly long vista, but can also obstruct circulation in the mall

PARLY 2, PARIS **37**

A mall cafe

38 SCARBOROUGH TOWN CENTRE, TORONTO
A mall seating and eating area

39 WOODFIELD MALL, CHICAGO
A carpeted seating well

There are several arrangements which can be used to make the mall areas more interesting. For example, they should terminate at spacious courtyard areas, often successfully planned in front of major department store 'magnets'. Large floor areas can be broken up with sunken courts in which special events can be arranged, and another device often used in French centres is to incorporate attractive eating areas in the malls such as that at Parly 2, Paris. Enclosed malls are superb *37*
locations for boulevard-type cafeterias if the Fire Officer can be persuaded to accept them. Naturally, the French excel in the design of them, and they have produced some exciting solutions. They can rarely be planned as an afterthought and both space and service requirements must be built into the mall design. *38*

It must not be forgotten that foot for foot, the internal public mall areas are the most expensive part in the centre to build, heat and maintain. Commercially, therefore, it is essential to ensure that the mall volume is not allowed to increase beyond that which can be justified for valid reasons.

An attractive and functional feature not so far widely used in the UK is the sunken seating well. If carpeted it *39*
can provide a colourful feature and is sufficient to provide adequate short term seating for shoppers without being too attractive to the habitual layabouts.

The planning of space below staircases and escalators *40*
requires careful detailing if an unsightly empty area is to be avoided.

WOODFIELD MALL, CHICAGO **40**
A seating area: a good use of dead space below escalators.

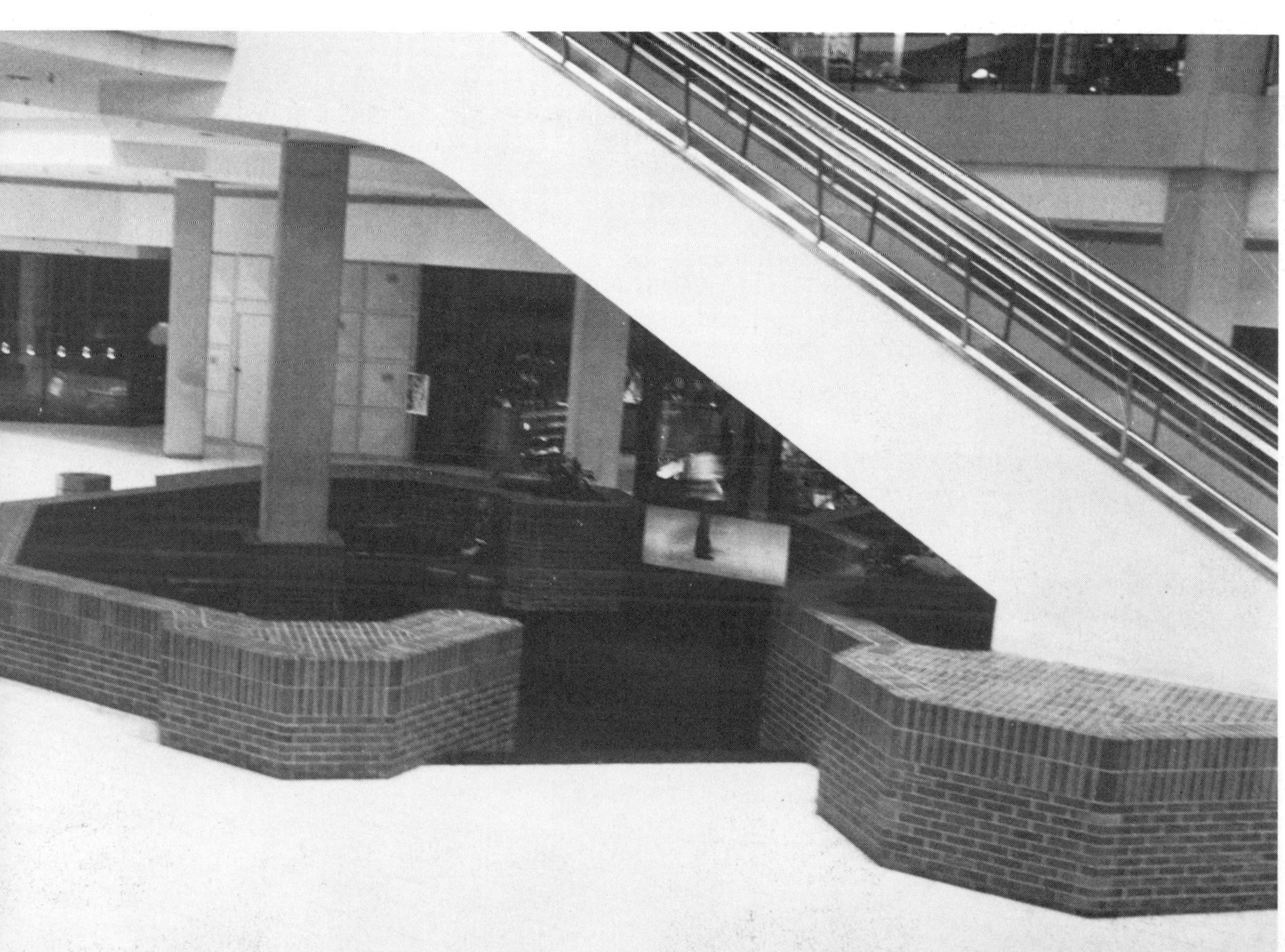

Lighting

41 If the centre is to be enclosed, the lighting levels need to be carefully considered. There is a wide range to choose from, for they can vary from mainly natural lighting to a low level of artificial illumination relying mainly on the brilliance of the shop fronts.

With the former, such as in the main square at Midtown Plaza, Rochester, and the malls of Yorkdale, Toronto, there is a distinct difference in character between their appearance in the day-time, when the square and the malls are dominant, and in the evenings, when the shops burst into light and take precedence. With the latter, such as at Place Ville Marie and Place Bonaventure, Montreal, the centres have the same character at all times.

What should be aimed at in the shopping areas is a mellow level of illumination, but not necessarily the same level throughout all parts. An overall evenness can appear monotonous and will not take advantage of the opportunities that exist to highlight certain areas; on the other hand, harsh lighting effects will detract from the pleasant atmosphere which is the aim of the centre.

Wherever natural daylighting is used, it must be controlled, so that apart from overcoming problems of solar gain, disturbing variations of cloud cover and sun brilliance are avoided. Where very bright areas are provided, say in internal courts, they should be so designed as not to dominate the surrounding shops.

Careful gradation of illumination at the entrances is essential, particularly if a low level of lighting is selected inside the centre. Even on a dull day, the street will be brighter than the malls, and the shoppers' impression, until their eyes become adjusted, will be one of relative gloom.

Chandeliers and special lighting effects are best used with discretion and certainly should not visually dominate the shopping areas. Bright light sources should be screened, for there are few things more disconcerting to the shopper than to be suddenly dazzled by a spotlight. Concealed reflective lighting has much to commend it, for it can provide warm, soft and discreet illumination, subtly setting off the design of the mall areas without detracting from the importance of the shops.

41 *A variety of ceiling and lighting treatments*

41a VELIZY 2, PARIS

POINTE CLAIRE, MONTREAL **41b**

An effective mixture of daylight and artificial light

EASTGATE MALL, HAMILTON, ONTARIO **41c**

41d GRIGNY 2, PARIS

41e VICTORIA CENTRE, NOTTINGHAM

ROSNY 2, PARIS **41f**

42 GRIGNY 2, PARIS
A seating arrangement in an out-of-town centre; but, because of the likelihood of damage to the fabric covering, unsuitable for a downtown centre, where it might attract vandals and layabouts.

43 YORKDALE, TORONTO
A simple but serviceable seat design

ELDON SQUARE, NEWCASTLE UPON TYNE **44**
An integrated rubbish receptacle and seating feature

Purpose designed telephone stands: **45**

SCARBOROUGH TOWN CENTRE, TORONTO **45a**

ELDON SQUARE, NEWCASTLE UPON TYNE **45b**

Furniture

The main problem in the selection of all shopping centre furniture is that whilst it must of course be pleasant in appearance and fit neatly into the overall aesthetics, it must have the minimum possible maintenance costs. These costs will be high if furniture cannot be easily cleaned and is not vandal-proof. The more delicate and often more attractive materials can be used only with the greatest discretion.

Shopping is tiring, and if the shopper is not to complain, some seating is essential. Seating areas need to be readily accessible from the main shopping areas but should not obstruct them. They can, for example, be pleasantly planned under staircases, particularly if the floor level is slightly sunk, as at Woodfield Mall, Chicago. Very simple arrangements can often be satisfactory, such as the broad steps around the central area of this centre which are much used by the weary shopper.

Seats need to be substantial in construction for they *42*
will be well used and are very prone to vandalism; but if they are too comfortable, shoppers will stay too long and layabouts will have to be moved. A 10-minute seat would be ideal!

The simple seating at Yorkdale, Toronto has *43*
withstood ten years of heavy use very well, but the more appearance-conscious fibreglass seating at Sherway Gardens is bulky and uncomfortable, and takes up valuable mall area.

Shoppers deposit a considerable quantity of refuse, and a large number of litter bins in both shopping and seating areas is essential. Their satisfactory design presents considerable problems. They need to be large but not so large that they are difficult to empty. The method of emptying needs to be simple and quick without the use of special tools, and it is best, although not essential, if the deposited rubbish is hidden. The use of plastic liners can make emptying quicker and avoids the need for frequent washing out, but they create some fire risk from cigarette ends, are not always readily obtainable and involve continuous replacement cost. Metal perforated-liners do not need replacement but are heavier and severely limit the bin container size.

There also needs to be a generous provision of ash *44*
trays. They can be incorporated in the litter bins, but this will almost certainly complicate the emptying procedure. Sand-filled ash trays can look attractive, but they involve high maintenance costs. Simple naturally finished metal trays which can be easily emptied and wiped out are to be preferred.

The provision of some public telephones is desirable. *45*
Some developers are not very sensitive about the use of the standard Post Office telephone booth, which they are prepared to accept despite its rather incongruous appearance within a shopping mall. The simple

off-the-shelf hood may be acceptable; otherwise a special design is necessary, particularly if the booths are to form a design feature in the mall. It has been found that a developer can make a small but useful profit from these telephones if, as is normal, he rents the equipment from the Post Office.

46 Adequate direction signing is essential, but if it is overdone the shopping area can appear cluttered. On the other hand, the signs must be readily visible when needed and give clear, concise and consistent information. They should be provided when the centre is opened when they will be most needed, and not added as an afterthought when the initial influx has subsided and frequent shoppers have found their way around. Some form of correctly orientated indicator board illustrating the layout of the centre and the disposition of the various traders is useful near the entrances. Models are expensive and difficult to alter when letting changes occur, and easily replaceable plans can prove much cheaper.

An enquiry desk is often desirable within the mall area; a suitable location should be selected and the connections provided for necessary telephones and public address systems.

Unrestrained advertising within the centre can spoil the environment and can tend to compete with the retailers' display. Limited advertising can sometimes be contained in carefully designed features which may also have some other function — such as a centre plan directory.

47 It is worth-while providing some play sculptures in areas off the main shopping routes. They need to be
56 specially designed to minimise the risk of injury, but they do attract the children, who may possibly therefore encourage their parents to visit the centre. Unfortunately, some coin-operated mechanical machines which are attractive to young children are garish in appearance and really need to be hidden away.

Planting can help to create a luxurious atmosphere in the malls and to soften the construction forms. Very realistic artificial plants and trees can be obtained and have been used, for example, at Parly 2, Paris. Their use should not be discounted for they avoid high maintenance and replacement costs, but they do involve a fire or smoke risk which might possibly not be acceptable to the Fire Authorities. Artificial lighting can stunt natural plants, but it has been found that by using wide spectrum fittings, luxuriant growth can be achieved.

All this furniture can be expensive; but it is false economy to provide cheaper and flimsy pieces, for they will not stand heavy use, and if the overall character of the centre is not to be down-graded, their replacement will involve more cost.

46 *Examples of well designed direction signs which are clear and do not detract from the overall decor:*

46a LE CARREFOUR LAVAL, MONTREAL

46b ELDON SQUARE, NEWCASTLE UPON TYNE

Examples of play features: **47**

VICTORIA CENTRE, NOTTINGHAM **47a**

LE CARREFOUR LAVAL, MONTREAL **47b**

48 *Fountains have a fascination for shoppers — but also for vandals, and therefore need careful protection:*

48a ROSNY 2, PARIS

48b ELDON SQUARE, NEWCASTLE UPON TYNE

49 VICTORIA CENTRE, NOTTINGHAM
Emett's 'Aqua Horological Tintinnabulator': a feature which is popular with shoppers of all ages. (See also front cover.)

SCARBOROUGH TOWN CENTRE, TORONTO **50**
The glass-sided lift

Special features and symbols

In order to attract the shopper to the centre, it is as well to provide special features which they are unlikely to see elsewhere.

Sculptures can possibly help; but as well as being fairly expensive they are generally static and seldom add anything to the liveliness of the atmosphere.

Fountains, on the other hand, can provide an *48*
attractive chuckling background noise, and when carefully lit can give a special sparkle to particular areas. There are many possible attractive arrangements, but care must be taken to avoid the problems of splashing, which can often be overcome by using the gentle waterfall principle. Detailing of the fountain edge needs careful attention if it is not to become a seating ledge. In spite of its vulnerability to vandalism, some form of water feature is usually worth-while.

Various forms of mobiles are sometimes used, such as the perspex tubes at Rosny 2, Paris. They can help to highlight an area, but if stationary they are simply decorative: their routine is soon finished and the shopper's interest soon lost.

A more expensive but attractive type of feature is the animated type, such as the Clock of Nations at Midtown Plaza, Rochester, and Emett's 'Aqua Horological *49*
Tintinnabulator' at the Victoria Centre, Nottingham. With their half-hourly programme of mechanical movement and music they can be fun in themselves and give the children something to show the visiting grandmother, as well as providing somewhere to meet and something particularly special to the centre. As with fountains, they can be fairly delicate, so special precautions are necessary to protect them against vandalism.

Another type of special feature can be one that involves some unusual way of doing something fairly normal. An example is the glass-sided cantilever lift at *50*
Scarborough, Toronto. Although it provides a slower means of communication than the adjacent escalators, it is useful for disabled persons, it is a fun ride (there is always someone waiting to take the trip), and again (at least in that area), it is peculiar to that centre.

The design of a symbol for the centre can greatly *55*
assist in providing this special identity. It can be used not only within the centre itself but also in conjunction with the advertising and promotion campaigns, and it really becomes the house sign, which is particularly helpful during the opening period when the centre is seeking to establish itself. The design of such a symbol is a specialised exercise, but it can extend the centre image beyond the physical confines of the buildings and its use should be adopted wherever possible. In town centre schemes it can provide an opportunity to relate the centre to a local historic, commercial, industrial or artistic association.

Some centres have commissioned purely abstract or artistic designs, and these also have their place, but it must be recognised that they are less likely to be appreciated by the vast majority of shoppers visiting the centre than a symbol reflecting local or historical connections.

Flooring

51 The selection of the flooring material in the public areas involves the often conflicting claims of appearance and maintenance. Appearance is to some extent a matter of opinion, but undoubtedly a warm colour in the pale-yellow to brown range can provide a pleasant background. After the shop fronts, the floor is the most noticeable surface, and so there is some advantage in ensuring that there is no visual competition as occurs at Rosny 2, Paris. On the other hand, subtle changes of floor colour can break up what might otherwise be over-large areas.

It should be remembered, particularly when a lower level of illumination is selected, that the floor can become the major light-reflecting surface. In this case, a light tone is essential.

The problems of maintenance are really caused by the need to select a surface which will withstand the necessarily frequent cleaning operations and minimise the effects of the inevitable chewing gum and dropped ice cream. This tends to lead the choice to some jointless impervious material; terrazzo and marble can offer these advantages, together with an acceptable colour range.

If somewhat higher maintenance costs can be accepted, floor tiles can offer a wide range of colours and particularly attractive finishes can be provided in the buff to brown range. Where not used consistently through the centre, this type of finish can be adopted with advantage to highlight some special trading area such as a food arcade. Tiles will prove quicker and cleaner to lay and have fewer problems of quality control. One of the problems with this material, however, is that it is hard and tiring on the feet, particularly if the jointing is uneven. Nevertheless, it avoids the creation of dust just before completion, and areas subject to wear or damage can readily be replaced at night with the minimum of inconvenience.

Rubber sheeting does not offer a real alternative, for it is difficult to clean and the black ribbed matt type is depressing in appearance.

The provision of carpeted areas should be seriously considered, for they can provide a pleasant and softer character, but of course they need frequent cleaning and replacement. If subject to heavy traffic, even the heaviest duty carpeting is unlikely to withstand wear and tear and retain its appearance for longer than a couple of years.

51 *Types of flooring. Detailing at junctions of different flooring materials needs careful treatment to avoid cleaning problems:*

51a *Tile & terrazzo*

51b *Brick & terrazzo*

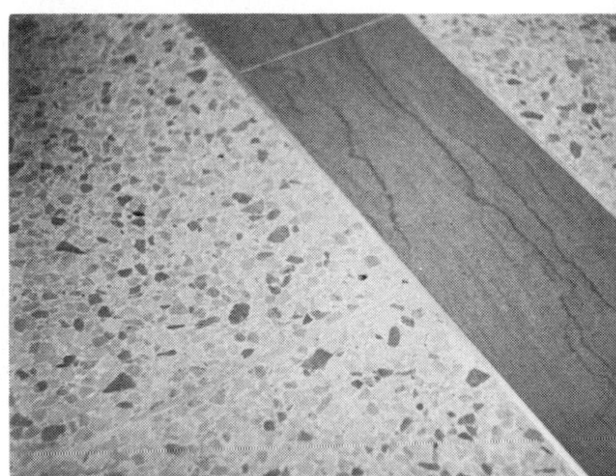

51c *Marble & terrazzo*

51d *Tile & carpet*

Whenever different flooring materials are used, it is essential that special care is taken in the detailing where they meet, for the same cleaning machine cannot necessarily be used for both, and damage can often occur.

Shop Fronts: interior design and control

The positive approach

Although there may be some exceptions, in the main the standard of design of shop fronts and interiors in the UK falls well below those to be found, for example, in the average shopping centres of North America and France.

If full advantage is to be taken of the potential offered by a shopping centre complex, the developer has to take a positive approach to ensure that the shop units are as attractive as possible. The shopkeeper has to be encouraged to provide the very best unit he can and then to display his goods in the most attractive way possible. He will almost certainly feel he knows his business best and will not take kindly to the view that many members of the shopping centre team, dealing as they will with a large number of tenants, may have much wider experience of different solutions and ideas. Those team members dealing with this aspect must therefore have been selected for their sympathy with and knowledge of the shop designers' problems. Careful selection of tenants can ease the problem and very often the stronger traders will be found to pay particular attention to their trading image; but clearly the best centres do not leave matters to chance.

Although there are a few situations where a standard shop front is applicable, perhaps in a particularly sophisticated centre, in the main such solutions lead to an uninspiring overall appearance and it is normally best therefore to try to provide as many exciting and different displays as possible. What is required is a framework within which the tenant's designer has the opportunity to exercise his skills and a procedure to ensure that he takes this opportunity.

The framework is possibly best set out in a pamphlet, which should succinctly describe the environment and aesthetic character of the centre and give clear guidance as to the shop front design philosophy looked for. It should state quite clearly those matters which are mandatory and those areas where original solutions will be encouraged. It is essential to ensure that this pamphlet gets into the hands of the retailer's designer and does not, as often happens, get lost in the shopkeeper's files; and it is also helpful if a meeting can be arranged with the retailer's designer to discuss the particular problems before he starts work. The pamphlet can usefully be extended (as is North American practice) to give the tenants guidance on a whole series of matters which concern them. A recommended check list of headings would be as follows:

Section 1 – Introduction

a Purpose of the handbook
b Outline description of the centre
c Names, telephone numbers and addresses of the development team
d Questionnaire to be completed by tenant, giving names of estate agents, architect, designers, contractors, solicitors, etc
e Publicity
f Programme requirements

Section 2 – Trading

a Lease terms affecting trading
b Merchants' Association
c Insurance

Section 3 – Design

a Lease terms affecting design
b Shop design controls
c Centre symbol and signs
d Standard specification
e Security
f Fire protection
g Building Regulations
h Tenants' check list – design

Section 4 – Construction

a Project management
b Names, addresses and telephone numbers of suggested contractors and suppliers
c Names, addresses and telephone numbers of local authorities and statutory undertakers
d Tenant's contractor's insurance.

The procedure adopted should give the developer the final decision of approval of the design, and when necessary, this right should be exercised. The approval system, however, can be extremely time-consuming, and it must not be allowed to degenerate into a repeated reject situation. As opening day approaches, further rejections are very difficult to justify commercially. It is often useful for the developer to provide a list of recommended designers who he is confident can be expected to produce solutions of the right quality, and the right to reject designers not on this list who cannot be seen to meet the required standards can in the end save everybody time and money.

It is worth bearing in mind that in North America very often the developer will have the right to employ his own designer at the tenant's expense if the designs are not approved to a contractual timetable.

At all events, there should be a procedure for submission, and when unsatisfactory proposals are received, a meeting should be arranged between all interested parties with the clear intention of reaching a

52 CRETEIL
A modern French centre, planned on classical American proved principles. This centre has a fine collection of shop fronts, and the food shops are collected together in one area.

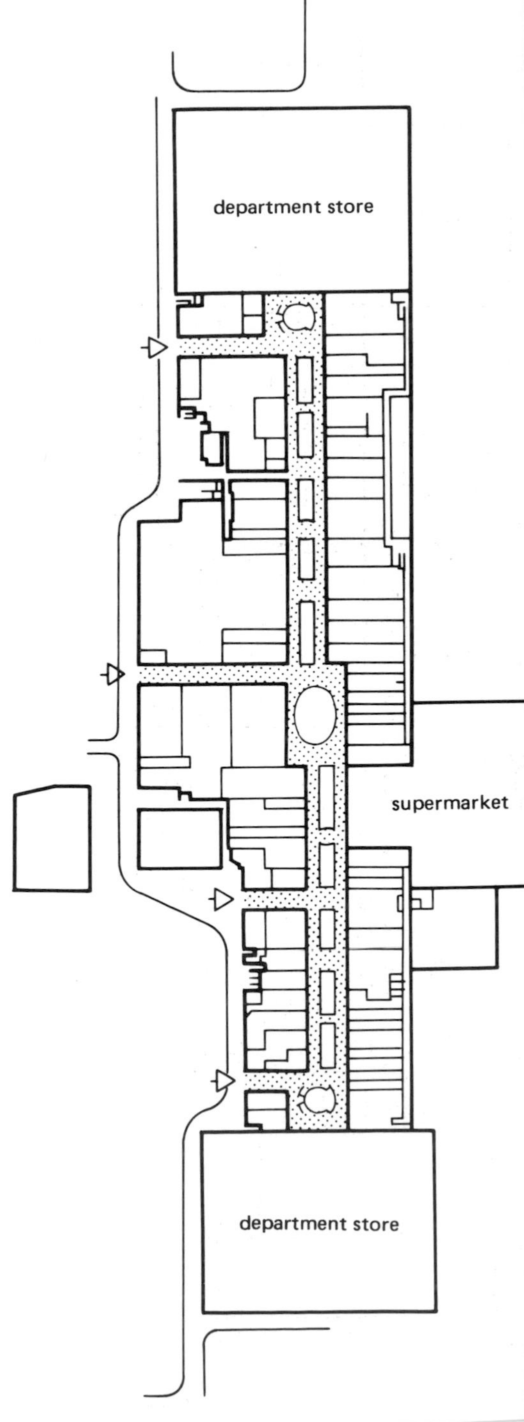

52a CRETEIL – upper level

mutually acceptable solution. This can often involve a lot of travelling time and use a lot of tracing paper, but in the long run, it will prove quicker and more fruitful than lengthy telephone conversations, long letters and yet another rejection.

CRETEIL – lower level **52b**

Fascia design and lettering

Probably one of the most inhibiting restrictions on exciting shop front design is the traditional high street shop fascia, being in the order of 1 metre (3 ft) high, and together with the normal glass line of around 2.75 metres (8 ft), representing well over a quarter of the total shop front area. *53*

If the designer has to work within this 2.75 metre height, he has little scope for providing the exciting and original designs looked for, but if the traditional arrangement is discarded, he immediately has a much greater freedom.

In principle, therefore, the use of a fascia should be discouraged and the designer should be encouraged to use the whole of the front area in some special way. If, however, a fascia is unavoidable, then it is as well to have it regulated, offering a selection of heights from which the tenant can choose the one most suited, otherwise the centre will have a messy appearance overall.

Shop tenants often take the view that a large amount of wording is necessary to describe their business; but within the overall centre complex a clutter of lettering will look unsightly, and the tenants should be restricted to one descriptive name, be it the company's name or a business description. Only in very special circumstances should any additional lettering be permitted, and then only a small amount and much smaller in size.

It is possibly of some interest to note that it was reported (*The Times,* 21 October 1974) that for a period W.H. Smith changed their name on their Kingsway London branch to 'Sims' and found that apparently no one noticed. The real usefulness of the tenant's name in the fascia must therefore be suspect. A case could conversely be made that since no one looks, it does not matter what is provided, but clearly the better designed centres avoid the clutter of excessive lettering.

There are inevitably different views as to how much control over lettering should be exercised. It may take the form of certain approved heights set on a standard horizontal base line or on a standard horizontal centre line; but these arrangements have the disadvantage that lettering with a sloping base does not really conform, and there is greater scope for the designer if less rigid rules can be applied.

A better arrangement probably is simply to restrict the length of sign to, say, 75% of the shop front width (if horizontal) or to 60% of the height (if vertical), to stipulate the maximum sizes of letters – say 0.66 metres (26 ins) if letters are to be of different heights – and to stipulate that the sign panel is at least 0.3 metres (12 ins) wider than the largest letter in the sign.

One thing is certain, however: in the overall concept of the centre it is important there is some cohesion, and this is readily destroyed if startlingly different forms of projecting signs and lettering illumination are permitted. Except in special circumstances where they form part of some overall design concept, it is as well to prohibit projecting signs.

With regard to lettering illumination, it has been found that a satisfactory effect can be achieved if only
53 back-illuminated or halo-lit lettering is permitted. It is important that the lettering illumination does not distract the eye from the shop merchandise, and particularly garish effects will result if only one or two shops have back-illuminated fascias, as is often permitted in the Paris centres. The particular tenant may be highly delighted, but the dominance he achieves will detract from the overall appearance, and if all the shops have them, then they will distract the shopper's eye.

On the other hand, it is also important to insist that all shops adopt whichever form of lighting is decided, for in the same way that a dead length of frontage will lose a shopper's interest, so a shop without illuminated lettering will break up the overall continuity.

The lettering itself can cause problems. Individual house styles should be accommodated wherever possible, but if they are not well-designed they should be rejected. It is as well to remember that if the site is right and the centre well-planned, the good tenant will be as keen to take space as the developer is to have him, and only gentle persuasion may be needed.

The design of a new alphabet is a very specialised exercise, and it is normally better to select a universally accepted face, though every design and proposal has to be considered on its merits. Naturally, the design must be suited to the trade, and it is usual for the more sophisticated fashion traders to go for the most imaginative forms. Good taste, quality, design flair and style are of paramount importance.

53 *An example of back-illuminated lettering*

WOODFIELD MALL, CHICAGO

VICTORIA CENTRE, NOTTINGHAM

LE CARREFOUR LAVAL, MONTREAL

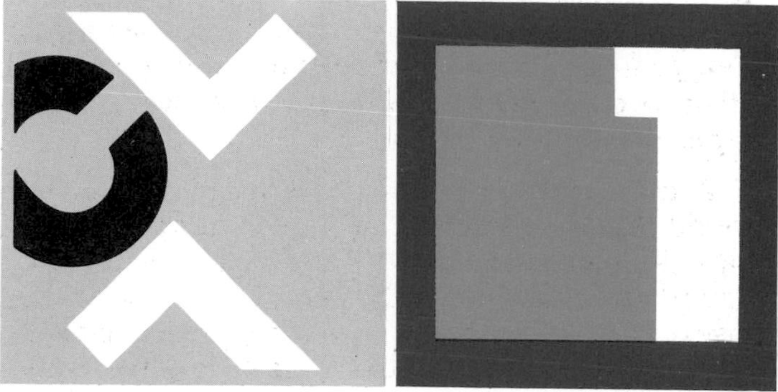

SQUARE ONE, MONTREAL

SHERWAY GARDENS, TORONTO

SCARBOROUGH TOWN CENTRE, TORONTO

ELDON SQUARE, NEWCASTLE UPON TYNE

PARLY 2, PARIS

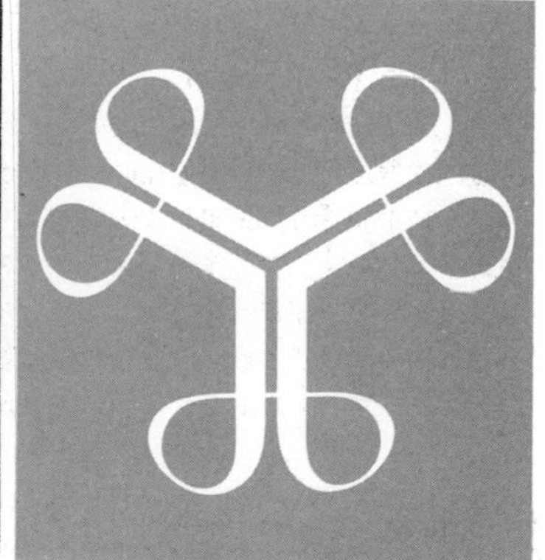

YORKDALE, TORONTO

Examples of centre symbols **54**

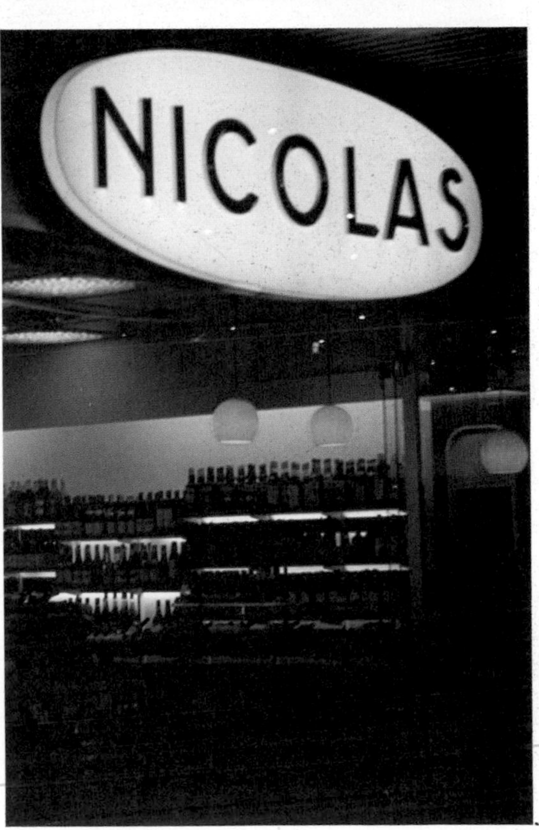

55 *Examples of shop fronts and fascias*

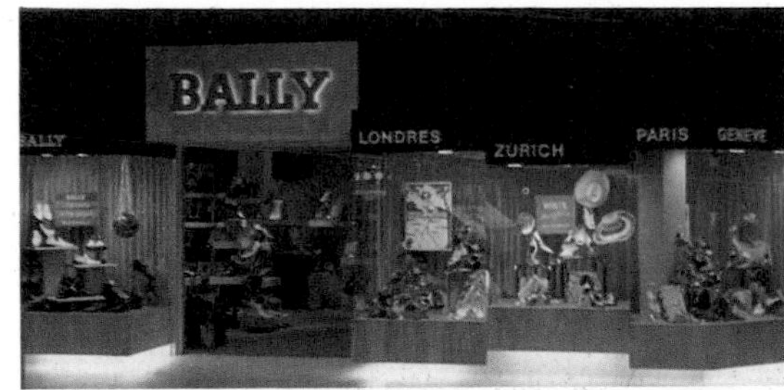
BALLY
BALLY
LONDRES
ZURICH
PARIS
GENEVE

mia

MODESTY

BOUCHARA

Madigans

mobilia

Miss Selfridge

FRANCE BONBONS

DIFFERENT CIRCLE

56 ROSNY 2, PARIS
Colourful play feature

Shop fitting and merchandise display

In order to achieve a highly successful centre, it is important that the developer's interest does not stop, as is normal, with the shop front. He should be equally concerned that the unit is attractively fitted out and the merchandise well displayed, for he should have aimed at providing a balanced set of traders, and a poorly finished unit with an inferior merchandise display will affect and lower the overall standard of the centre. Indeed, with an open layout the inside of the shop becomes the shop front.

With the multiple chains, it is normally fairly easy to check whether the standards which will be provided will be satisfactory; but it is essential that the chain clearly indicates which of their various categories is contemplated, for otherwise a lower standard than expected may materialise. Even large stores can sometimes misjudge the balance of trade, to their cost when they subsequently have to up-grade the store.

Greater problems, however, can be anticipated with the local traders. To achieve the highly desirable full range of tenant mix, their representation is essential, but they often do not really understand the difference between high street and shopping centre trading. Their understandable inclination is normally to provide a minimum quality to suit their purpose, but this attitude must be overcome.

The developer is well advised, therefore, to retain some right of approval of the internal shop fitting works for these reasons alone, as well as to ensure that the works and services will be compatible with the centre's systems. This does not mean that he should insist on expensive materials and finishes. There is, of course, a minimum quality required, but it is the overall atmosphere and attractiveness which should be the prime criterion.

On one study tour of some North American centres in which a number of traders took part, it was very interesting to note that although they were not particularly impressed with some of the sales techniques, they were universally attracted by the exciting use of colour. The shopkeeper's aim is really to catch the shopper's attention, then to show her the goods, and then to encourage her to buy. It is questionable whether some of the devices to capture her attention have a place in shopping centres — loud music, excessive use of posters, bill stickers and flashing lights, for instance. Some shops provide very bright lights in their window displays, but in this energy-conscious age this can be expensive, and can cause ventilation problems in a commercial centre environment. One easy method is the selective use of colour, and very attractive effects can be simply achieved with paper and card.

The importance of merchandise display cannot be over-stressed, for the whole shopping centre problem has been concerned with finding ways to lead the shopper gently to the shopkeeper's goods. Poor display techniques will waste the opportunity so carefully provided.

Multi-level designs

The theory of multi-level solutions is now better understood, and this arrangement can be adopted with some confidence. Nevertheless, certain disastrous UK examples clearly indicate the dangers that exist. A multi-level solution should therefore really be adopted only if the full implications are understood and analysis has proved it to be the correct solution.

The introduction of the third dimension means that a successful pedestrian flow pattern becomes more difficult to achieve – and it is hard enough to arrange in a single-level centre. The multi-level arrangement should therefore really be considered only if the required shop area is too great to be accommodated astride a simple 200 metre mall arrangement, or if the value of the land is so high that retail space maximisation is essential.

As with the single-level centre, the basic principle must still be to achieve a high level of pedestrian flow by balancing the 'magnet' traders and the entrances.

Possibly the simplest examples to illustrate this type of arrangement are the North American out-of-town car-orientated centres such as Woodfield Mall, Chicago, and Scarborough, Toronto. These are surrounded by vast car parking lots, and it is a relatively simple exercise to move sufficient spoil to position the entrances from car parks so as to provide both upper and lower shopping levels with equal shopping potential. The Brent Cross Centre has been planned on this principle.

In order to achieve a balance of trading potential, shop tenants should be arranged by the mix-policy to encourage inter-communication, and with advantage the larger 'magnet' stores should locate their similar departments, such as women's fashion areas, at different mall levels.

Initially, there is both a problem of providing a balance of trading potential and traders on each floor and a need to encourage a movement of shoppers between the floors, and the more levels provided, the greater the risk that these will not be achieved. The shops at each level should therefore be as readily visible as possible from the other levels, and so the provision of open wells is essential and the use of glass or metal grilles as balustrades almost mandatory.

This visual inter-connection between the floors can be considerably improved by careful detailing of the mall section such as at Creteil, Paris, and the Four Seasons
57 Mall, Greensboro, Carolina.

57 FOUR SEASONS MALL, GREENSBORO, NORTH CAROLINA
The mall is tiered on either side, which tends to reduce the mall volume while greatly increasing the exposure of shops to both levels. The lower mall shop fronts undulate in and out in relation to the face of the balcony above, which reduces the potential tunnel effect at this level.

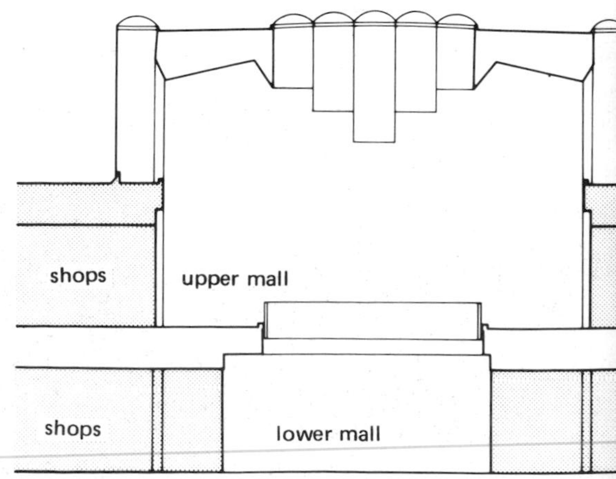

Once the shopper has been made aware of the other levels, there must then be some readily available means of getting there. As a prime method of transport, lifts have insufficient capacity and stairs require too much energy, although a reasonable number of easy-going stairs must be provided throughout the centre as a secondary means of access.

Ramps and travelators can be provided, but to be sufficiently easy-going as to encourage their use, they will need to occupy a considerable area. The provision of escalators therefore becomes essential.

When carefully sited, escalators can considerably enhance and extend the pedestrian flow to areas which would otherwise be away from peak trading locations. Escalators are, however, expensive, so there is some pressure to reduce their numbers; and anyway, an over-provision could result in a loss of trading potential in the extremities since these areas could be too easily by-passed. Because of this expense, they are often not provided in areas immediately adjacent to department stores, the principle being that this will encourage shoppers into the store who will then pass through it to another mall level. However, this solution should be adopted only with caution, for if the store escalators cannot be seen (as is often the case with this arrangement), the shopper will not necessarily enter the store and so will not cross to the other level, at least at this end of the mall.

One of the relatively recent developments in multi-level design is the use of mezzanine or half-levels, as for example, at Woodfield Mall, Chicago. The physical change from one floor level to another is *58*
materially less, and steps and ramps much shorter, than between two full levels, so that they become more readily acceptable to the shopper, who is induced to move to a different level without using an escalator or staircase. It is still essential to avoid 'dead ends' and to ensure that these intermediate levels will generate a reasonable pedestrian flow.

WOODFIELD MALL, CHICAGO **58**
An example of the use of mezzanine or half-levels

8 Complementary activities

Residential use

At one time there was considerable pressure to redevelop central areas in such a way that the centre would remain alive after the shops and offices had closed. Experience has clearly shown that despite theories and protestations to the contrary, the presence of flat tenants living above shopping centres has little effect on the evening life of the centre. Although there may be valid reasons for using the air space above a shopping centre for residential purposes, it must be recognised that this may well increase the cost of the centre by lengthening the time for completion of the building contract. In any event, care must be taken to ensure that the residential development does not aggravate the problems of centre management by having common means of access, for to achieve adequate security, to avoid unnecessary vandalism and to facilitate cleaning and maintenance, it is desirable that the centre should be closed at night and at weekends. Residential and other complementary forms of development should not prevent this.

Office use

Office developments can often be successfully integrated into shopping centre developments. In a central area scheme they can sometimes tip the scales to produce a viable development, and in extremely valuable locations they can be the primary source of income from the development. One of the most outstanding examples of this is Place Ville Marie in Montreal, which is essentially an office complex of some 42 storeys with a system of pedestrian shopping malls at ground floor and basement level.

This concept of forming covered shopping malls below office developments is one which is being extended within the central areas of some Canadian
59 cities such as Montreal to provide a series of pedestrian links to key parts of the city. Every opportunity is thus taken to exploit the retail potential of the pedestrian flow so created. These subterranean pedestrian ways make good shopping arcades and are particularly suited to the climatic conditions of Canada, where sub-zero temperatures persist for much of the winter.

In such mixed developments it is essential to establish the priorities to be given to the various types of use. In the Montreal Place Ville Marie development, the shopping was primarily intended to meet the needs of the offices. In most central areas the retail development will receive preference and the office plan will have to give way to the planning requirements of the shopping centre.

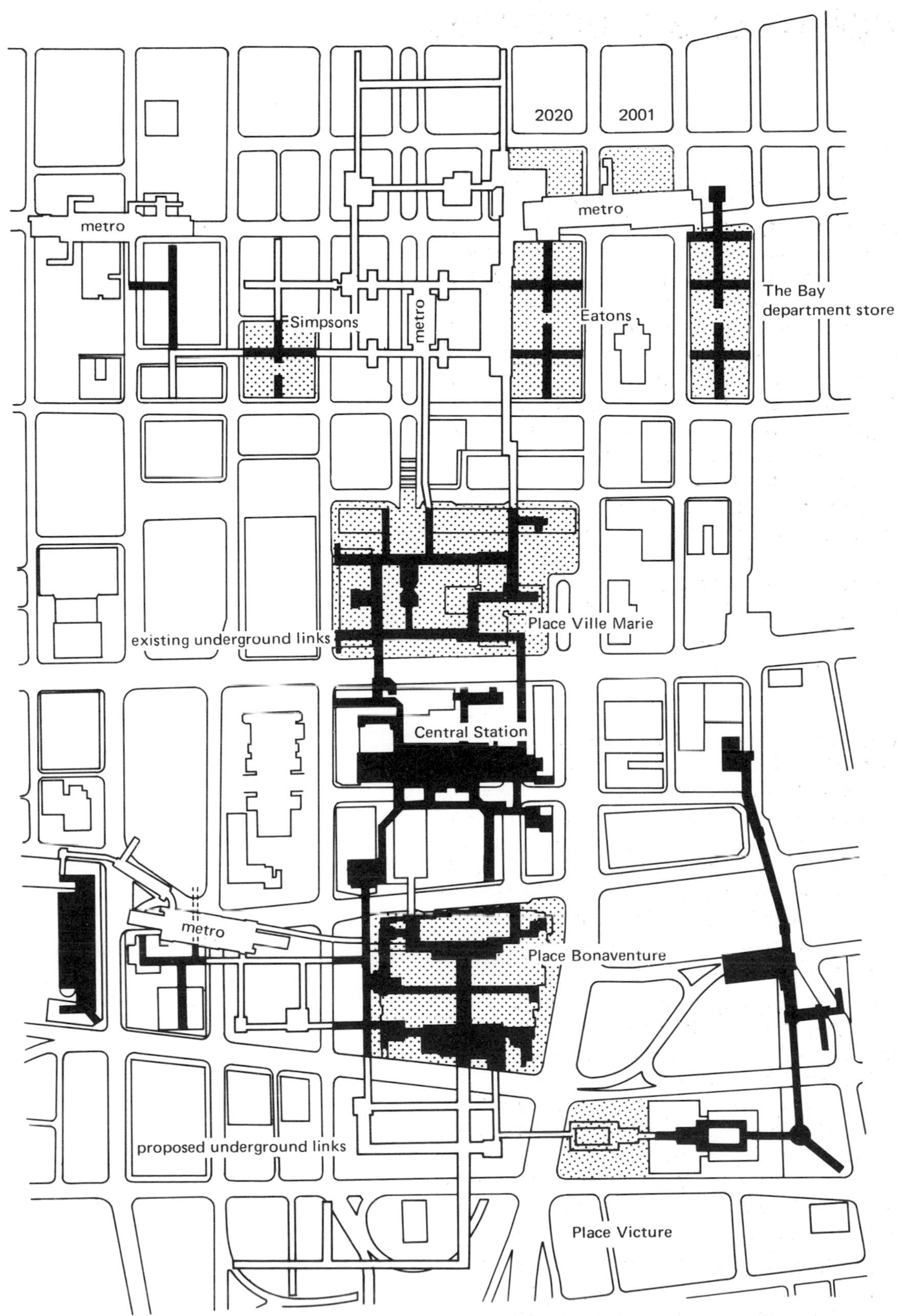

CITY CENTRE, MONTREAL 59

A map illustrating the extensive underground pedestrian links being developed in the city – an attractive feature in a region with extremes of climate, and with a shopping potential which is being exploited.

Leisure use

A number of leisure and recreational uses can be readily integrated into a shopping development, with the following possible benefits to the centre:

- i Such uses attract potential shoppers and thereby stimulate pedestrian flow
- ii They encourage family visits to the centre, thus making shopping a family activity
- iii They assist in providing interesting and useful activities within the centre after normal shopping hours.

Leisure operations such as cinemas, recreational
60 centres, ice rinks, bingo halls, beer kellars, public houses, discotheques and libraries can be successfully incorporated into a shopping centre development. It must be recognised, however, that the economics are such that these operations can normally be introduced only if subsidised by the development or by the local authority. Furthermore, careful consideration must be given to the possible management problems created by conflicting uses. These may include such matters as cleaning difficulties, increased security problems, extra costs of providing centre services and greater exposure to vandalism.

60 ELDON SQUARE, NEWCASTLE UPON TYNE
The recreation centre

Catering

Catering is not so much a complementary activity as a vital part of a successful centre. All too frequently in the UK its importance has been under-estimated by both developers and retailers.

If shopping is to be recognised as a pleasurable activity which the housewife and the family wish to enjoy, it follows that the shopping expedition to the regional shopping centre is quite distinct from the brief weekly visit to the supermarket. The length of time the shopper spends in the centre is often a measure of the degree of enjoyment which she derives from the shopping expedition. As an encouragement either to visit or to prolong a trip to a centre, attractive catering facilities must be provided. Although the shopper may not have the benefit of an expense account, it does not follow that he or she will be content with the rather basic fare offered by the average snack bar or cafeteria restaurant.

A recent development in North America has been the
61 collecting together in one area of a number of fast-food operators, each serving food at a communal eating area. These have proved very attractive to the shopper, and even with their higher cleaning and maintenance costs they provide an overall rental income comparable with the main mall shop units. It seems unlikely that the larger catering companies in the UK would be interested in organising such an arrangement – and they may indeed be unsuited for this type of operation. To ensure

61 *Catering*

61a GOURMET FAIR, SHERWAY GARDENS, TORONTO
A plan of the communal area where food is served and eaten

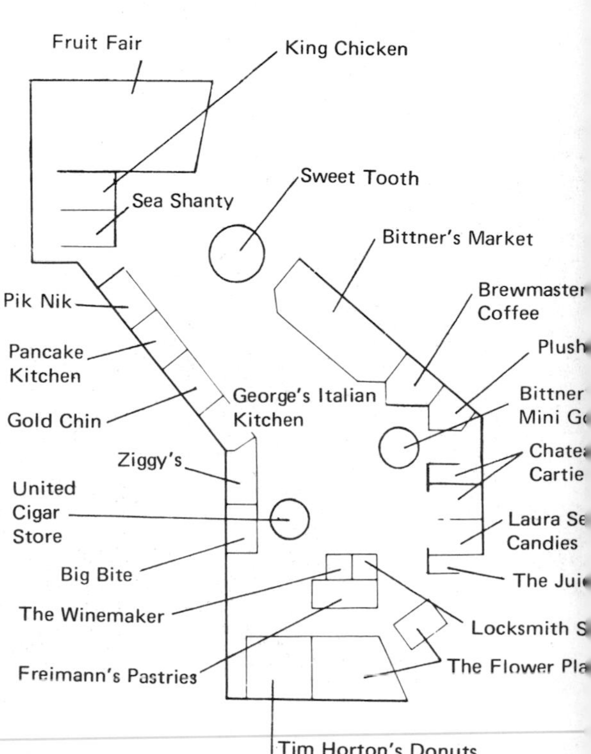

that catering units are well managed and kept spotlessly clean, the operation should be kept under the direct control of the centre manager.

To be really effective, however, catering units must not be considered merely as a way of using some unwanted back area. They need to be integrated into the overall plan at a point of good pedestrian flow.

Catering cannot be left to chance: it is not a trade to be included only if the letting agents happen to produce a caterer just before the centre is due to open. It must be carefully planned and located early on to ensure that the most appropriate catering facilities can be offered to the shopper.

Since the provision of eating facilities is so important in making the centre attractive, and since catering of the right quality is so difficult to achieve, it needs to be accepted that where the operator cannot afford to pay a rental competitive with other retail traders, the unit will need to be subsidised in one way or another. This is a good example of the suitability of a rental based on the trader's turnover.

Cafe in a pedestrianised street in Munich **61b**

9 Accommodating the private car

Although due weight must be given to the current concern for energy conservation and the general interest in bulk transportation systems such as Park-and-Ride, it is unlikely within the foreseeable future that the general public will willingly give up the individual freedom of movement bestowed by their motor cars.

By driving to a regional shopping centre the shopper can enjoy the consumer benefits of competitive prices coupled with the economy of being able to complete the shopping expedition without further travel. As shopping becomes increasingly a family activity, the motor car is probably no more costly than public transport, with the added convenience of door-to-door travel and the ease of carrying bulky goods.

If a shopping centre is to trade successfully, it is essential that the shopping public can obtain easy access to it, and a generous parking provision immediately adjacent to or within the centre will encourage them to visit it. North American practice for their out-of-town
62 centres, which are almost wholly dependent on car shoppers, is to think in terms of 5.5 parking spaces for every 1 000 ft^2 of retail area. There is only one out-of-town centre in the UK, although if others were planned, comparable standards would need to be contemplated. However, since our centres are unlikely to depend entirely on car shoppers, a provision in the order of 3 to 3.5 spaces per 1 000 ft^2 is a more reasonable target.

62 GALERIES D'ANJOU, MONTREAL
Shopping centre and car park

At the Victoria Centre, Nottingham, where parking space is also available outside of the centre, some 1 650 parking spaces are provided for a gross leasable area of some 780 000 ft^2. There it has been found that the parking spaces are over-subscribed on peak trading days when around 5 500-6 000 car visits are made, and a smaller number of longer visits will occur at Christmas. However, a balance has to be achieved; for clearly it is uneconomical to provide a capacity to meet occasional peak demands. If traffic congestion on access roads is to be avoided, car parking provision should be planned in relation both to the capacity of the access road and to the availability of alternative means of transport.

Shopping centre parking should, of course, be provided for the shoppers and not for the general public. It must therefore be controlled and parking dues should be arranged to encourage the shopper, whose stay will last about one to three hours, and not the commuter. The longer stay should therefore be very expensive. As a matter of interest, a census at the Victoria Centre, Nottingham, showed that around 60% of the shoppers stay less than two hours, leaving a sizeable percentage who do indeed stay for a longer period.

Internally, car parks should be planned to provide an easy parking search pattern and a separate direct exit route.

The method of parking payment will affect the space requirements at entrances and exits if long back-up queues are to be avoided. With large car parks as at Hamburgher Strasse, Hamburg, and Midtown Plaza, Rochester, there is some advantage in arranging for payments to be made at the link with the shopping centre so that once the shoppers get into their cars they can leave the park with the minimum delay; but this arrangement does involve greater management costs.

Very large car parks can involve complicated search patterns and serious congestion at the exits. These exits need to allow half the parking capacity to leave in a 30-minute period, so when more than five or six hundred spaces are provided it is best if they are arranged in separate areas or buildings, with some link arrangement to combat overflow problems.

The following points have been learned from experience by most developers and may be worth noting by those embarking on a major car park associated with a shopping centre:

i If it forms an integral part of the shopping centre it may need to be ventilated and provided with sprinklers. This is a very heavy capital cost.

ii Clear direction signing within the car park needs to be carefully worked out before opening.

iii Lighting consultants and contractors are apt to recommend an excessively high standard of illumination. Ignore their protests and put in the minimum you consider necessary. The electricity bill will still be a heavy burden.

iv Never install heating in car park ramps unless you have a cheap source of electricity. Occasional heavy loads will be very expensive on a peak demand tariff.

v Whenever possible, retain control over the running of the car park to ensure that shoppers are not discouraged from visiting the centre by a badly run car park. (Incidentally, it is worth considering the employment of female car park attendants, as they can be more efficient and more courteous to the shopper than their male counterparts.)

The structural requirements of car parks are different from those of the shopping centre and it is invariably more economic to provide them in separate buildings. It is good practice to locate car parks so that the users have to pass into the shopping centre. It is, for example, highly undesirable in down-town locations for potential shoppers to 'escape' into surrounding areas without discovering the 'delights' of the shopping malls. The link with the shopping areas needs to be carefully planned if advantage is to be taken of its real pedestrian flow
63 potential. One connection link, such as at Midtown Plaza, Rochester, is possibly the ideal. Certainly numerous links should be avoided and these links should not be entirely dependent on a lift system. Wherever possible, a simple pedestrianised connection should be the objective.

A useful facility in the parking area, particularly for department stores, is the provision of a parcel pick-up point. Once having made a bulky purchase – which may be the main reason for the visit – the shopper is then free to walk round the centre and need not return to the car, when she might be inclined to take the parcel straight home.

63 MIDTOWN PLAZA, ROCHESTER
One of the few examples of an American downtown shopping centre. Opened in 1962, it marked a milestone in shopping centre development. The centre was built on the space between the existing department stores.

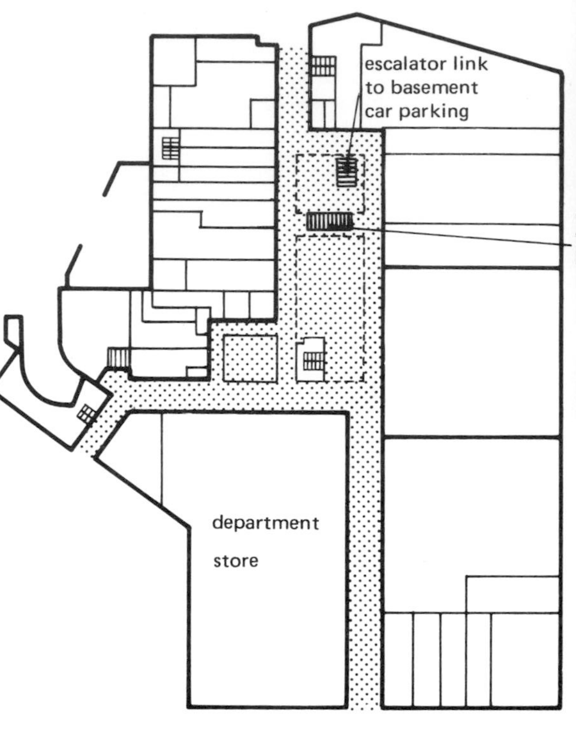

64 CRETEIL
The shopping centre and car park

10 Single activity centres

Hypermarkets

Hypermarkets and discount stores are often thought to be an unreasonable threat to the regional shopping centre. Hypermarkets are essentially large scale food supermarkets which have expanded their range to cover most convenience goods (food, toiletry, newspapers, cleaning materials – generally purchased on a weekly basis) as well as some comparison goods (clothing, furniture, household goods); but the range of goods offered, the accompanying service, the shopping environment and the dependence on car transport are not usually comparable with those available at a regional shopping centre. The hypermarket, in fact, is more likely to pose a threat to the supermarkets and the neighbourhood shopping centres within the same catchment area.

Discount stores

The discount store usually takes the form of a department store which sells its goods on supermarket lines, offering very competitive prices and a minimum of personal service. In America, in fact, these stores have traded alongside and within shopping centres for many years. Stores such as K Mart, Woolco, Zeller, Towers and Shop Rite are well known and offer the American shopping public the choice of shopping in one type of environment or the other. Many shoppers are attracted to the comfort, convenience and quality of the shopping centre, fully aware that they may be paying a few cents more for some of the goods – rather in the same way that some shoppers in the UK like to shop in quality stores such as Harrods. Like the hypermarket, therefore, the discount store is not a significant threat, and in some cases may indeed be integrated into the shopping centre to provide the attraction of a bargain basement facility where this is not provided by one of the normal department or chain stores.

However, the discount store often needs to be located on the periphery of the centre to minimise problems of car park access and trolley recovery. The American practice is to locate discount stores in separate buildings in the car park where they cause little inconvenience and pay a minimal rent. In Canada and France, on the other hand, the preference is to locate discount stores and allied convenience trades at one end of the mall or in a short side mall with a special character.

11 The design and construction process

The design team

This subject will be covered in greater detail in a later publication on project management, which is of course an essential development tool for the efficient and effective control of the team of consultants and contractors involved. Nevertheless, the following comments may be useful.

The developer

It must never be forgotten that if the centre is to be commercially successful it is essential that the developer retains overall control during planning and construction and ensures that his experience is applied. He will place the final result in jeopardy if he allows the consultants to take charge. If the developer does not have the experience of a successful centre behind him, then he would do well to unite forces with one who has.

It may be wondered why a consultant cannot achieve the same results as a developer: and in some cases he may be able to; but consultants do not have quite the same financial incentives. The developer will make a profit only if his centre is successful, whereas the consultant does not carry the same risk, except to his reputation, and even eminent architects have been known to build enormous white elephants.

The architect

Invariably this is the most difficult selection to make in respect of enclosed shopping centres, where the experience of UK architectural practices is limited, and the size and sophistication of these centres may well restrict the choice to larger firms. The developer must, moreover, recognise at the outset that it is unlikely that any member of the architect's design team will have worked previously on such a centre.

Although the architect will invariably be the principal professional consultant, he will nevertheless be a member of a development team which will include either the client or his agent. It is essential that he accepts both the need for team working and the client's co-ordination and control overall. Whilst the architect will tend to see design solutions in architectural terms, it is the responsibility of the developer to interpret the likely reaction of the shopper, as well as to ensure that the design is functional in management terms. For example, the Emett Water Clock at the Victoria Centre, Nottingham, has proved a resounding success with shoppers of all ages and is now part of the local scene. Though, in fact, Emett was employed on the architect's recommendation, a more normal architectural solution may have been a work of art or sculpture which would simply not have been appreciated by the majority of shoppers.

Design consultants

There are three types of special design consultancies which are worth considering: one a general appointment, and the other two for specific aspects of the work.

To consider the general one first: as indicated under the section dealing with the architect, it is quite likely that his practice will have little, if indeed any, practical experience of the design of covered shopping centres. It is very important, however, to ensure that the design team includes someone with a deep knowledge and understanding of shopping centre operations, who can fully appreciate the problems facing the developer and letting surveyors. It has been found, moreover, that this type of consultancy, which can avoid the pitfalls, is useful not only through the detailed design stage but even more so during the initial concept development, when what is needed is a precise analysis of the layout problem and an ability – with aesthetic appreciation – quickly to suggest arrangements which answer the problems of space utilisation, pedestrian flow, disposition of major space users, entrances and so forth. If the team is weak on experience, the appointment of this type of consultant has much to recommend it, but it is important to ensure that the consultant and the architects will be able to work well together.

The specific design consultancies worth considering are for the public mall areas and the signs. As mentioned previously, North American experience often tends to the view that the design of the public shopping areas is such a specialised problem that the employment of a specialist designer is warranted. If the right man can be found, such an arrangement should not present any particular problem, for he would be employed in the same way as, say, an interior designer for a hotel or a special suite of offices. In addition, for a centre of any size, it would be just as well to employ a graphics consultant to design and co-ordinate the multitude of signs which need to be integrated within the overall concept, including the centre symbol mentioned earlier.

Other consultants

The selection of other consultants presents less of a problem. Where a service consultant is employed, experience of shopping centre problems is desirable, and it is preferable for the developer to have his own in-house specialist to advise on heating, lighting, air conditioning standards etc, so that the benefit of experience on previous schemes for both design and maintenance can be utilised.

All consultants, and particularly the quantity surveyor, should be employed by the client (usually the developer) so that there is no doubt as to whom they should report. Employing professional consultants as sub-consultants to the architect or possibly the engineer is not to be recommended.

Site representation

It is prudent to discuss the question of site representation and control at an early stage: consultants are much more amenable to establishing a site team if it is discussed during the initial negotiations. On a major project it is desirable that there should be an adequate professional team full-time on site to supervise and control the construction operation. Monthly or even fortnightly visits are unlikely to suffice, except in the case of relatively small, straightforward contracts.

If the client wishes to attend the architect's site meeting as an observer or to hold his own meetings, this should also be clarified at the outset.

Terms of appointment

It is in the interest of both client and consultant to spell out the terms of appointment in some detail instead of relying entirely on the normal professional fee scale and Conditions of Employment. Both clients and their developments often have their own special requirements. Similarly, the consultant's design programme may need consideration, and if much travelling is contemplated, the control of expenses may be a significant factor.

ELDON SQUARE, NEWCASTLE UPON TYNE **65**
Play and seating features

12 An approach for the successful planning of shopping centres

The sequence of operations

There is considerable room for a re-assessment of the sequence of operations which should be adopted in the UK. It has been fairly normal practice to begin by briefing the designer to prepare plans, which are then used to obtain a planning approval, followed by commencement of building works, sometimes even before the major tenancies are agreed. The number of centres of mediocre design, however, gives a clear indication that this procedure cannot guarantee success, for the problem is considerably more complex than simply building and letting space.

Unfortunately, because there are relatively few centres built, there is (despite protestations otherwise) a shortage of specialist expertise and what is offered is often superficial. This is not to say that there are not good consultants: quite clearly there are first-class architects, engineers, quantity surveyors, valuation surveyors and letting agents; but their knowledge is very specialised in their respective fields and will not separately provide the proper framework to develop a shopping centre with any guarantee of success. What is needed is a framework within which these experts can be organised so that their knowledge is available when it is wanted, neither too early nor too late; and this framework should ensure a proper work sequence which will provide an evaluated solution backed by research, data and experience in the minimum time and with the minimum cost.

A sequence which enables checks for viability to be made at the end of almost every stage is as follows. (The importance of these viability checks must always be remembered, for if the economics do not work they have to be corrected or work should stop.)

Stage 1 — Initiation

The first task must be to assess the possibility of acquiring the land and the probability of obtaining town planning permission. This can normally be quite satisfactorily carried out by the in-house staff of the developer — whether the developer is a private company or a local authority.

Stage 2 — Potential and suitability

In assessing the potential, a number of considerations need to be weighed, and the American practice of carrying out an economic market analysis has much to recommend it.

Such a study should include:

- i Identification of catchment area
- ii Analysis of future population trends and income projections within the catchment area
- iii Analysis of family expenditure within the catchment area
- iv Survey of population within driving distance and public transport catchment area
- v Study of types of major and speciality stores most needed in the area
- vi Analysis of the effect of the projected centre on the existing trading pattern in the area
- vii The proximity and effect of competing shop areas within the catchment area
- viii Analysis of sales/volume potential foreseeable over, say, a ten-year period
- ix Assessment of retail floor area requirements in the proposed centre.

These statistics should clearly indicate whether there is a shopping need for a new centre. Very often it will be obvious that a site has shopping potential, but without this information this potential cannot be accurately gauged.

Whilst the results of economic surveys should be treated with some caution, it must be concluded that a plan based on a combination of a practical evaluation of facts and theoretical survey is most likely to be founded on the best possible assessment. Under certain conditions where towns are isolated from the influence of neighbouring communities, calculations of shopping demand can be more reliable. The research department of an organisation such as the John Lewis Partnership is able to forecast with a good deal of precision its likely turnover, even in an area where it is not currently trading. Planners and developers would often be well advised to consult leading retailers, who can give sound advice on trading potential.

In assessing the suitability of a site, consideration will need to be given to:

- i Accessibility of public transport systems
- ii Nearness and accessibility of major road networks
- iii Availability of public utilities
- iv Suitability of the land for building.

It follows that the questions at this stage are really: 'What is the profit potential of the site?' and 'Will a shopping centre satisfy the needs of the developer, the tenants, the local authority and the community at large?' It is the function of the market analysis, backed by assurances as to the physical suitability of the site, to provide the answers to these questions.

Normally, the only out-of-house consultancy necessary is from a specialist economic market analysis organisation.

Stage 3 — Size of gross retail area

The aim of the next stage is to assess in some detail the gross retail area to be provided, to decide whether it is to have one, two or more shopping levels, and to obtain an intermediate check on viability.

In order to achieve this, what is needed is an appreciation of the site area and its general configuration, an assessment of the quality and type of trading to be provided — obtained from the conclusions drawn from the market analysis — and some knowledge of the requirements of the planning authority as to access and parking. In this connection, local authorities and planners could usefully liaise with both developer and retailers before reaching a firm conclusion on the appropriate retail area.

Regard must be had not merely to the total retail area but also to the nature of its make-up. A large department store can occupy more floor space than the total floor space required by all the other standard units in a centre.

As the analysis is still at a theoretical stage and all the design criteria are not yet known, preparation of detailed drawings is unnecessary; there are further important aspects to consider, and once plans are prepared they too easily become a fixed basis, psychologically difficult and probably impossible to discard.

At this stage it may be desirable to discuss initial building cost estimates with the quantity surveyor, but not necessarily so if sufficient in-house expertise is available. At all events, it must be for the developer to set the cost budget for the project and he must not allow the consultants to override this responsibility.

Stage 4 — Type and character

In the past, the trading character of a shopping centre has often been haphazardly found out only at the end of the day, when tenants are sought to occupy the space. This is highly unsatisfactory, for without an early assessment of what trading level will be desirable and aimed for, neither rental levels nor the developer's income can be accurately calculated, and financial forecasts are largely blind and certainly not as accurate as they should be. It is therefore necessary at this stage to decide what the character of the centre will be, and whether any special feature should be aimed at, as this will affect potential trading (and thus rental) levels. For example, a basic decision is necessary as to whether or not the centre should be covered or air-conditioned, and a relatively simple cost analysis exercise at this time will indicate whether these features can be afforded.

Other decisions have also to be taken; for example, whether the centre should be of the classical American long straight mall type or, say, a much more intimate, closer-knit layout as might be more in keeping with the centre of an older town like York or Bath; and what physical appearance and environment should be aimed at. In a new town a futuristic design approach might be proper, whereas in a town like Windsor, something more suggestive of the history of the area may be appropriate. In other words, it should be decided what design character is most appropriate and whether or not a 'theme' mall should be provided.

These decisions need to be made at this stage because they will affect the rental levels which will be achieved. Different types of tenants and shoppers will be attracted to different types of centres, and the rents affected accordingly. If a definitive point of view is not taken now, it is unlikely that it will be made until the final drawings have been prepared, and a change can then only be made, if at all, at the considerable expense of time, effort and money. These decisions are the responsibility of the developer, for only he will have a complete appreciation of the final concept.

With the present-day mood of public participation, consultation with local pressure groups is often desirable. The power of these groups must not be under-estimated; often, unless due note is taken of their views during the early stages of the project, considerable frustration will arise, and indeed the proposals can be and sometimes are abortive.

Stage 5 — Preliminary breakdown of space users

As part of the previous assessments, it is probable that the number, size and type of department stores required will already have been decided. If not, they should be fixed at this stage, and so should the numbers and types of major space users. At the same time, a conscious decision should be taken as to the desirability of including any specialist areas, such as a retail market, 'Gourmet Fair', 'Shop in Shop' or similar specialist trading areas — perhaps an important location for a group of exclusive fashion shops or a minor wing for antique or book shops. Every new shopping development really needs to offer at least one feature which is special to it. Lack of consideration of this point may be the reason why so many UK centres are criticised for being soulless and uninspiring.

Once the major and most important elements have been decided, it is then relatively simple to break down the gross retail area into a schedule of smaller shop units and assess their number, type and size — and then, of course, cross-check against the major space users selected to ensure that no imbalance has arisen. At this time, if not before, a decision should be made whether a turnover rent lease will be adopted, as such a decision will affect the tenant mix layout.

If in-house expertise is not available, the break-down of retail areas can probably best be done by the specialist experts used to provide the economic market analysis. The work is still at the theoretical stage, but a realistic appreciation of the designer's brief is being gradually evaluated.

Stage 6 — Selection of tenants

Once the size and type of centre has been assessed and a general appreciation of the accommodation required has been gained, the next stage is to select the key tenants for individual units. So far as is known, this has never been carried out early enough in the UK and its importance can best be appreciated when it is realised that the one single factor which could guarantee a successful centre is the strength of its traders. A superbly designed centre with poor tenants will be a commercial disaster, but a badly designed centre with good tenants may still be a financial success.

The policy must be to attract a strong and balanced set of traders, and the developer at this stage should decide whom to approach and begin discussions with prospective tenants as soon as possible. The aim at this stage is to produce a realistic letting picture — a prudent exercise for the developer, as he will soon discover the likely strength of his centre. Several shopping centres in the UK which turned out to be almost complete disasters would never have been built if this precaution had been taken.

Unless there is an in-house expertise, it will normally be necessary to obtain a letting agent's advice at this time; he must, however, be sympathetic to the tenant mix philosophy.

Stage 7 – Schematic layout

At last, with the basic research and analysis completed, it is possible to consider a plan for the centre. There should by now be a clear appreciation as to the content, environment, character and level of trading to be aimed at.

It may well be and indeed probably is best if the development surveyor now sits down with the designer to explain what is wanted, so that together they can translate the requirements into rough layouts. There are always alternative solutions; they should all be examined and the final selection made only after the advantages and disadvantages of each have been fully weighed.

It is possible again that the developer will have sufficient in-house expertise to prepare a schematic layout: although probably, since there is a need to visualise in three dimensions, a project architect or designer should also be involved.

Stage 8 – Selection of tenant mix

Once the basic dispositions have been settled, the plan should be developed to include the preliminary tenant mix proposals. When the necessary adjustments have been made, then and only then do detailed layout plans serve any useful purpose.

There is, of course, much work still to be done, but it can now be based on a framework which will offer a considerable guarantee of success. The designers, quantity surveyors, engineers and letting agents can all be clearly briefed as to what is required of them, in the knowledge that their contribution will fit into an overall scheme based on an in-depth analysis of the requirements of the development.

In North America certainly, best practice has shown that the most successful projects are those where the developer consciously makes the basic decisions and carefully selects consultants who can skilfully interpret them.

Stage 9 – Development of solution to completion

The later sequences need not be described in such length, for they are concerned with the normal procedures of building operations. Basically they involve:

- i Finalisation of land acquisitions
- ii Receipt of town planning and Building Regulation approvals
- iii Completion of drawings and specifications
- iv Placing of contracts
- v Building operations
- vi Completion of any outstanding lettings
- vii Completion of project.

There are, however, one or two points worth mentioning.

First, during this sequence, effective project management will save both time and cost (as indeed it will with any building operation). There has to be someone with an overall control ensuring that the consultants and builders are proceeding, that materials are arriving in the correct sequence and that costs are being kept within the budget; and it needs to be appreciated that the separate consultants employed, whilst working successfully in their own fields, will not have a broad enough view to ensure that all the parts are necessarily coming together in the proper order to the developer's best interest. The best person to look after the developer's interest is the developer himself and he is at risk if he fails to take this responsibility.

Secondly, with shopping centres of any size, very serious problems can arise when tenants move on to the site. It is often at this time that the main contractor takes the opportunity to claim for delays. The tenants' shop fitting works need to be organised, and it will pay dividends if the developer appoints a clerk of works to supervise these operations, deal with tenants' problems, such as making arrangements for temporary services and refuse disposal, and indeed ensure that tenants' contractors are on site and will be ready to open on the right day. Retailers in the UK are often very disappointing in their failure to achieve agreed opening dates even when given very adequate time for shop fitting. Perhaps there is much to commend the American practice of requiring tenants to pay rent from the opening date, whether or not they are trading.

Thirdly, there comes a time when, no matter how brilliant the idea, the penalties of alteration are so severe that they really must not be accepted. The project management team will be able to advise at this point, but in principle no alteration should be permitted once building commences. If the initial pre-building sequence has been properly carried out, such changes should not be necessary to assure the viability of the project, and these ideas should be left until the next development.

Completion of the centre as quickly as possible is, of course, essential and this means not only that the centre opens on time, but also that all those annoying inevitable defects are efficiently corrected. The project management team should remain involved until the Schedule of Defects items have been fully completed.

66 ROSNY 2, PARIS
An attractive display of fruit and vegetables, possible only in an enclosed centre

13 Conclusions

In some documents the conclusions may be the only part that busy people have time to read. So far as this publication is concerned, this section is certainly not intended to be an alternative to reading the remainder. Nevertheless, it would seem clear that over the past decade a few important factors have emerged, each of which is important, if not vital, to successful shopping centre development. They may be summarised as follows.

The role of the local authority

It is difficult to see a major shopping centre scheme being undertaken in the UK in the future unless in partnership with the local authority. The enthusiasm and co-operation of the local authority is an essential ingredient.

The landlord and tenant relationship

In a shopping centre operation landlords and tenants tend to become active partners, each working for the same objective – the success of the centre.

Lessons learned

A number of planning principles and design techniques have been learned from recent experience which is readily available. We must not make mistakes which can be avoided by undertaking adequate research and following sound advice.

Effective development management

Co-ordinating and controlling the planning, letting, funding and construction of a large shopping centre requires an efficient and experienced development team. The difference between good and indifferent management can easily account for a saving of 10% of the building cost and possibly some months in extra development time.

The importance of tenant mix

Perhaps tenant mix is the most vital factor in achieving a successful shopping centre, yet it is possibly the one about which least is known. A complete tenant mix policy has rarely been applied in the UK because of our tendency to leave lettings until development is nearly complete, and possibly because of our reluctance to use leases related to trading turnover.

Good centre management

Few shopping centres in the UK reach the standard of management which is now normal in most North American centres. Unfortunately, many British shoppers have little respect for tidiness and will discard litter on to the floor in preference to a rubbish receptacle. Nevertheless, there is no alternative to good cleaning, good maintenance and efficient security in a successful centre. We have to accept that high standards will be achieved only by a determined, skilful and experienced management organisation.

Environment

Shopping centres are for shoppers, and it must never be forgotten that the whole purpose of the exercise is to provide a centre with an environment which will attract and please the shopper, who more than likely will be the lady of the household.